D1573137

A
MODERN
DUNCIAD

Richard Mason

Richard Nason

A
MODERN
DUNCIAD

The Smith　✦　New York

for Ruth

To the Rt. Hon. Harry Smith, Esq.
Poet, Publisher, and Patron

Prologue

Good Harry! Should you deem this too much praise,
Then read these Popeless couplets, noteless lays,
And contemplate how fears of too much fame,
Through faults herein not yours, flush out as shame!
Remember, I as poet, you as patron,
Can't quite escape the grip of that great matron,
The Goddess Dullness† we all hail as mater,
Who tripped up Pindar, Pound and Walter Pater,
And placed her offalled paw of failed intent
Upon the noblest efforts nobly meant;
Who wrought the strong and weak alike to rage
And weep to watch her vacuum suck each age;
Who hounded Dryden, Swift and Master Pope
To Hell and back, and Coleridge to dope;

---

†During the age of Pope (1688-1744) Dullness signified much more than mere tedium or lack of brilliance. It stood for an aggressive tastelessness, a bumptious grossness that bored, offended and demeaned at one and the same time, and unto death! In keeping with the classic temper of the time, Pope personified Dullness as a mock goddess. She in turn bred and fostered Dunces. For Pope, the greatest of the Dunces were the appointed Laureates of his day. Only Wit could negate the powers of Dullness, and satire was used to keep the Dunces at bay. See Pope's *The Dunciad* (1728).

Whose presence spell-like on these Spangled Shores,
This vacuum alters all, good air abhors,
And leaves within her vapid, smiling train
The self-inflicted deaths of Plath and Crane;
And who may now these plodding strophes precede
And hobble tropes whose only hope is speed,
Who though I would confound her still upends
My purpose with impoverished amends
That bid you, friend, since poets are forgiven,
Pin all these faults upon the age we live in!
    And, so, forgiven, if we do in fact
Accept this challenge leaving few intact:
To take our Goddess Dullness' awful measure,
And risk a finger up her place of treasure!
Those bards who sow and reap by whom they know
Will match this Divine Dullness blow for blow
And follow any ivied, crannied rut
To tip the till of Yeats' 'raving slut,'†
Whose body spray, though labelled 'Scent of Honey,'
Is Essence of Y-M-H-A and Money!
From pillow, post to periodical,
Too oddly really for this chronicle,
Those sports who work her carom-cornered trade
Have several heads, as hoe, and rake, and spade,
More hats than that, as teacher, critic, poet,

---

†A mound of refuse or the sweepings
    of a street,
Old kettles, old bottles, old rags,
    that raving slut
Who keeps the till . . .
                    —W. B. Yeats, "The Circus Animals Desertion"
Yeats saw the till-keeper here and elsewhere as the monitor of fame and
material gain, our own Dullness in one of her many guises.

And many funded chairs before we know it;
Anthologies ensue, and panels, boards,
As hand washes hand, those grants, awards!
Until, like bulbs in series, how they work it!
They beam as one upon the lecture circuit!
While, Harry, we, to shift a metaphor,
A tack by which such epics set great store
(Resuming Pope's serene, Augustan measure,†
Which we will stretch or snap for extra pleasure),
With only Fox and Stephanile beside,††
Must plow upon her all-devouring tide,
And set against her wild and toppling gales
Our Presses fragile as Phoenician sails;
And still not chase her with a dozen ryes;
Nor box our compass by her doubtful thighs!

    Not yet at sea, I still am overwhelmed
To undertake a course that Pope has helmed
So deftly even now his name alone
Inspires the dream of whelping life from stone,
As when the canny midwife of his Wit
Exclaimed upon the method he had hit
To make the madman and the Dunce his mark
And struck Heroic Verse from all that rock!
Since Homer led to Virgil, he to Pope,
and Pope to us, now we for further scope

---

†Johnson formalized the age of Dryden and Pope as the Augustan Age (Caesar Augustus) because of its appeal to the models and standards of antiquity. Pope's *Dunciad* is a mock epic recalling both Homer's *Iliad* and Virgil's *Aeneid*.
††Hugh Fox, teacher and writer, and Felix Stephanile, writer and magazine editor, have both devoted long service to the small press movement. They have been especially adamant in their efforts to wrest control of the language from the deadening and self-serving hand of the triple threat teacher-writer-critic.

Must call on him for courage to surmise
How Dullness in her prime is cut to size,
And from the Night and Chaos of her form,†
Extract a Model here and there a Norm,
To mend the many goodly molds that broke
As Roman rose to Gothic, buckled as Baroque,
And brought these modern, Existential bards,
To find a Cosmos in their private shards;
These scribes who spawn as Gresham's†† poorer species,
To fashion Epics from such bits and pieces,
Reduce Augustine's City to a paste,
Opinion to mere form, and sense to taste;
Who find the sources for their greatest themes
In drainage manuals with mosquito schemes,
Gazettes depicting planes that never flew,
Or books for boys whose projects never grew;
It doesn't matter, be it how obscure,
So when recast as verse it hound us more;
Or better, books with pages still uncut,
As symbols of a Universe that's shut
Against intrusions from the present tense,

---

†Pope held that the Goddess Dullness had Chaos for a father and Night for a Mother:
"Dullness o'er all possess'd her ancient right,
Daughter of Chaos and eternal Night:
Fate in their dotage this fair idiot gave;
Gross as her sire, and as her mother grave,
Laborious, heavy, busy, bold, and blind,
She ruled in native anarchy, the mind."
††Gresham's Law: Bad money (or specie) drives out good.

Then hailed as great because they yield no sense!†
   Let's take this modern poet's wide ellipse
And pull it in a knot that never slips
And lead him through the streets of Cambridge, Mass.,
For throwing stones at Shelley's dome of glass:
We'll let his students get a look at him
And then we'll throw his empty book at him!
We'll chain him to the arch in Greenwich Village
To put an end to Eliotic pillage,
The wanton plunder of de Kooning's palette,
The verse effect of Op with melting wallet;
At Bard, we'll book him as a hideous felon
For drinking on his grant from Andrew Mellon;
At Berkeley, charge him thus: syntax offender,
Excess reflexive verbs, the neuter gender.
So many marvels will we soon retrieve
From cuffs that out-finesse a Chinese sleeve,
We'll find the pea beneath that walnut dome:
The trick is in the poet, not the poem!
   Those pedants who declare the age is dead
That ever needed Pope or Dunciad,
His couplet, now, too narrow for our space,
His measure, Newton's feet in Einstein's race,
Have been undone by Dullness' utter ruse,
Whereby she argues sense outlives its use,

---

†In the late 1940s, there was a report that two, I believe, Australian scholar-poets had cut up a manual on, I think, mosquito control and pasted the lines together to such apparent poetic effect so successfully that the result was accepted and published as a poem by a prestigious American poetry magazine. The report seemed plausible at the time. This period ushered in the now pervasive poetry of confusion, whereby under the guise of a wider "modern" comprehension, poems adorn themselves with gratuitous obscurantism. One of John Ashbery's most ambitious poems is called "The Instruction Manual," based on a manual dealing with a new metal. As for "books for boys," Ashbery

And that the Universe, by math so curved,
Entails us to deny the thing observed.
Since Space and Time, she soars, are relative,
And clocks regress with speed and rulers give,
We must expand this mathematic metaphor
To slow and shrink the mind so less is more.
Thus Dullness drapes the poets' lupine lies
In sheepskins of a scientific guise,
And deems those bards most surely up-to-date
Who can with crypto-science obfuscate,
Compose their poems from cold, remote relations,
Consigning mundane things to spatial stations,
Omit the mortal theme that won't be right
Unless divided by the speed of light;
Who, since a moral might arise in rhyme,
Write only poems that chirr and ping and chime,
Who hold that Fate won't damn us or exhort us
Because of all that science now has taught us;
That fire can't wither, ice won't scathe, that sex
Has no connection with an age complex,
That pity is passe and passion rank
In light of Fermi, Bohr and Max Karl Planck.
Hence Dullness, in the Summa of her error:
O, Ecce Homo, in a convex mirror!†

  Now, Harry, I have tried to set the stage,

---

says that his long poem, "Europe," incorporates several passages taken intact from a British children's book, "Beryl of the Biplane" by William Le Queux, which he found in a bookstall on a Parisian quay. Also, our Existential poets show a penchant for "books with uncut pages." This, from Ashbery: "The pretensions of a past will some day/ Make it over into progress, a growing up,/ As beautiful as a new history book/ With uncut pages, unseen illustrations."

†The title of John Ashbery's Pulitzer Prize-winning (1976) volume is *Self-Portrait in a Convex Mirror*.

Which broadens and congests with every age,
Until today it overturns the hope
To find a ready focus for its scope,
To cram it all within a wooden O,
Or nutshell, though our poets wish it so.
When Pope in Twickenham once pushed his quills,
The Wits would know it soon at shops like Will's,†
For even as he scratched, he was so near,
They say his feather tickled every ear;
While we today are scattered everywhere,
And though our presses gnash and bite the air,
The Goddess Dullness in her wide intent
By satellite controls the continent;
So we must quietly feed our Press this way
As if it were a fire on Guy Fawkes Day,††
And trust the world to know the work we've done
As Dullness leaves the hilltops one by one.
And since our arrows shot into the air
At random do not find assurance there,
I'll rein Pegasus by the Forge's††† spark
To keep this fiery Muse upon the mark.
From time to time, in falls from Attic grace,
I'll look inside and put you in the place
Of all those Wits who joked and drank at Will's
From stoups the totler Dullness never fills.

---

†Will's was a London Coffee House, a haunt of Pope and many other wits of the day.
††Hilltop fires are still used in England to commemorate Guy Fawkes' Gunpowder Plot to blow up the British Parliament, November 5, 1605.
†††Smith Publishing, at 5 Beekman Street in the Wall Street district, employs as its logo a hammer and anvil.

Good god, one lesson we have surely learned
From poets who have all the lucre earned,
That every clown should have his handy claque
Of friends up front to keep the show on track.
    So, I'll be dropping by for anxious pause,
A welcome touch of cash and some applause;
At Suerken's† over oysters, rolls and beer,
Renew acquaintance with your patient ear,
And be astonished by your Russian waiter,
That stain-encrusted, ancient alligator,
Whose voice alone could dent the Goddess' mettle,
And whose Martinis from the kitchen kettle,
Were she inclined to any self-abuse,
Would send her smoking on an ocean cruise!
    You, Harry, whose idea this challenge was,
Must be my whole support and half my cause;
Who sends me to the fray with glad refrain,
Must, if I buckle, brace me up again;
And whoso knows that men like Bolingbroke,††
Who spoke to Swift, to whom so few men spoke,
Were larger men than we with larger verses,
Will find such ratios reflect our purses.
And should our talents lack the epic trait,
The spread of Dullness now has grown so great,
So burst the girdles that contained her once,

---

†Suerken's restaurant is a City Hall area landmark. Its oysters are excellent.
††Lord Bolingbroke was a philosopher and politician. A friend of Swift, he was
also Pope's powerful mentor and ally.

Since greater Dullness breeds the greater Dunce,
Should we by only half of half succeed,
Our share of triumph will be great indeed.
To purify the language of the tribe†
Is not our purpose but to purge the scribe,
At least to rouse him with our urgent prod
Until he cries again for man and God!
Just Fox and Stephanile beside? O, Lord,
Forgive me, many more have come aboard:
Yes, lofty Heller with her upswept hair
And downcast glance, young Tolnay with his flair,
Van Brunt and Boxer, Ryan with elan,
And you, Old Smithy, with the ultra plan,
Bernard the saint who fills the crucial cask,††
Such hearts and minds now crowd upon the task:
Come, take a drink, a pen, and draw a breath,
And damn this Dullness whose embrace is death!

---

†"Since our concern was speech, and
  speech impelled us
To purify the dialect of the tribe."
            —T. S. Eliot, "Little Gidding," *The Four Quartets* (1942)
Eliot lifted the notion in toto from Mallarme.
††The references: to Anne Heller, Tom Tolnay, H. L. Van Brunt, Ray Boxer and Bill Ryan, all of whom are strong exponents of the U.S. small press movement. They often work out of the Smith offices. Sid Bernard is a zealous chronicler of current history, in addition to being Smith's associate. He is a known fanatic when it comes to keeping the office water cooler filled. Smith is one of the founders of the Alternate Press Movement and a past head of COSMEP (Committee for Small Magazines, Editors and Publishers).

BOOK THE FIRST

Argument

The Proposition, Invocation and Argument, beyond What is dealt with in the Prologue. The Early and Recent History of Dullness in America. The Reassertion of her Empire on our Continent. Her Control over the Flesh and Spirit of the Natives. The Perverse and Playful Nature of her Muses. How Dullness is afflicted by the Boredom She propagates. Through Destruction of the Moral and Emotional content of Poetry, She controls all Realms of Culture. Her Dullness spreads to Financial and Political Spheres. She uses Women's Liberation to advance her Ends. Chaos holds sway; Darkness impends; Oblivion is near. Her Strength increases at Attack. She cancels New World Hopes for Progress and Liberty. She touts old Rubrics to stultify the Public Mind. How the Peculiarities of Individual Poets serve to mask their Common Vacuity.

O, mighty mother, ancient Goddess, you,
Who, once in sandals, now in Gucci shoe,
Still bring our Bards, in great abounding hordes,
Before the Guggenheims, Exxons and Fords,
I sing! Say you, O, Existential scribes,
Who populate Parnassus with your tribes,
How reign again, by your connivance cursed,
Still Dunces numberless like Dunce the first;
Say you, how Dullness will, now that you've written,
Enslave this Nation as it did Great Britain!
　　Our Goddess in that once Augustan Age
Did so promote, propound the Dunce's page,
So plaster every mind, that few could tell
How first she came to us when England fell.
The Wingèd Horse flew back to Gorgon's chest,
Some say, was then refoaled and galloped west,
To fledge its pinions in a sky so rare
That nightingales alone could scale the air,
And stepped, as once on Helicon, with ease
Until pure Hippocrene rose through the trees!†
　　Then Dullness came, the Indians insist,
A giant Thresher in a Diesel mist,
That spurted blood and money from its side,
That crashed through rivers, climbed the Great Divide,
And shredded prospects of what might have been

---

†Greek myth held that Pegasus was formed from the blood of the monster Gorgon's wounds. With the stroke of its hoof on Mount Helicon, Pegasus caused the fountain Hippocrene to flow.

To all these busy, little, greedy men!
At this, our Goddess might have raised a brow,
But sovereignty was automatic now,
Our Colonies were such a slavish host,
So anxious for the sale of Soul and Ghost,
Her dream of Baptist heads upon a platter
So lacking any Johns to make it matter,
America so sluggish as her ward,
This Queen of Boredom was herself now bored!
    When Pope assumed he sent her home, upended,
She then, by double somersault, descended,
To drive all simple Dunces through the door
Where Cibber† to his folly went before,
And send that barren, Existential band
Of poets to the caverns of the Strand††
To place impressions in Burt Britton's book
To show, not how they write, but how they look;
And doom the Gotham's††† search for local genius
To borrow Sitwell's girth and Cocteau's leanness,
And then, bereft of all celebrities,
Import the ghost of Joyce to all its teas!
Or bid Bukowski, bard by drunken chance,

---

†As Court Laureate, Colley Cibber was the main butt of Pope's satire in *The Dunciad.*
††The Strand Bookshop is composed of many high-ceilinged cavern-like recesses. On its staff was Burt Britton, who eventually came out with a book full of drawn self-caricatures by all our writers, poets included, sometimes with coy, self-deprecating remarks appended.
†††The Gotham Book Mart in Manhattan has so far failed to find American poets who can stir up as much interest at its weekly teas as Edith Sitwell did in 1947 and Jean Cocteau in 1948. As headquarters for the James Joyce Society, the Gotham plays heavily upon the Joycean presence.

Invite St. Mark† to do St. Vitus dance,
And think that Schaefer beer in paper bags
Could ever take off Dullness and her hags,
Who hang their banners on the City air
To turn a hundred enclaves into one Rag Fair!††
She sallies forth, unchecked and undetected,
By all the radar Technic has perfected:
Poor substitutes for Spirit's piercing eye,
Electron scopes that bind both bacilli
And blinding suns to all but primal causes,
Pile weight on Matter from the Spirit's losses:
And yet, in Nature nothing is destroyed,
And Absent Gods are only redeployed;
The Good and Evil Science would abjure
Are Gods we may defy yet not ignore,
As Oppenheimer††† makes his late amends
To give the Means of Science back its Ends,
And Heaven's running battle with our Hell
Resumes as cancer in the living cell,
And Dullness, even as our light is spent,
Subverts the basis of Enlightenment!
We track the Goddess in her empire vast
To tell it all as Hamlet at the last,
In grim aside, or Daniel in the den
Once raised an arm so other, later men

---

†St. Mark's Church on the Lower East Side continues as a redoubt for zany poets like Charles Bukowski, whose readings are sometimes punctuated by beer cans thrown, presumably, at the Establishment.
††The seedy part of London, which Pope chose as the breeding-ground for Dunce-poets.
†††Robert Oppenheimer, pioneer of the atomic bomb, as Galileo before him, confronted the moral obligation of science to assume responsibility for the ends to which the State would apply its work. He demurred, on moral grounds, from manufacturing the hydrogen bomb, was banished as a latter-day heretic by Truman and Eisenhower and then 'repatriated' by John Kennedy.

Might gather to outnumber bitter odds,
And reinvoke the greater banished Gods,
To curb this Goddess, as her circling flounces
Hem in two-hundred-twenty million Dunces,
Who now, as she perfects McLuhan's medium,
Contracts this touch of self-inflicted tedium!
    Upon her throne, she stirred: "This cannot be,"
She balked, "my weapon boredom turned on me?
Through undue closeness, subjects that I rule
Have rubbed this throne into a Dunce's stool,
And this great Grossness, whence their love is born,
By reflex stretches me, as yawn does yawn!
I'll not have it! My Muses Four, I say,
Desist from writing 'list poems' for this day!†
Your Queen has need of you in greatest trial;
Her subjects more contagious grow the while;
Through some shared gene or plate of caviar,
She's coming down with their behavior!
Behold her symptoms; buttress your dismay!"
Then as she swooned, each Muse unbound a stay.
The Goddess rallied; then addressed them all:
"Self-Service, hold! Good Smugness, fetch my shawl!
Fair Sadism, greet my hand! O, dearest three!
The fourth? My favored, sweet Anality!
By all I've done, by what I've set in motion,

---

†'List poems.' These are short, spontaneous poems usually based on a recipe, shopping list or 'things to do' note addressed to oneself. They enjoyed a certain vogue in the late sixties and early seventies among the quainter women poets such as Sandra Hochman, who announced she wrote poetry the way ordinary people "get dressed in the morning." The Goddess Dullness apparently instructed her Muses to maintain their daily contribution to the world's store of banality by writing 'list poems' as a regular practice.

I am beset, as by some horrid potion!
I've caught the Existential poet's plague,
And labor less than honest, more than vague.
To questions as to place or time of day,
I answer only in a cryptic way;
Abstract responses to a world so near
Transport me to a total empty sphere.
I've plugged emotion to an optic scan
That amplifies the visual side of man;
So should you prod me, thus! I'll never holler,
But explicate upon my sense of color!
This ailment is perverse, I told you once,
And speeds up tenses with their goal response;
Thus when you serve me toast for Sunday brunch,
I shall be well along through Tuesday's lunch!
It's also odd about the time that's past;
Tonight I go to bed on Monday last!
The notion is: To do away with Now,
With What and Why, to elevate the How;
Not you, not I, not qualities, amounts,
Not *what exists*, but *how you see* that counts!"

    Her Muses then, aggrieved by her complaint,
Moved swiftly lest she choose again to faint!
Now four on one, they lifted leg and arm;
At breasts and thighs, they labored with alarm;

Self-Service poured a No-Cal at her side,
As Smugness read aloud from TV Guide;
While Sadism took a patent leather shoe
And slapped her ample backside black and blue,
And sweet Anality, so light and fair,
Enlaced with tender plaits her pubic hair.
"Avaunt and cease!" The Goddess was aroused.
"By Jupiter, whose prong I have espoused,
Now by your tucker, Tom, and by your bib,
I also am the Dullness of Fem Lib,
And must not fall unwomanly a prey
To crudities that I myself convey!
Now I, who made the woman poet's pages
As empty as the man's for equal wages,
Shrug off the poet's analytic fit
That turns all substance into puffs of wit!
I placed him in a solipsistic shell,
Wherein, like spermless eggs, his notions dwell:
'Yourself alone is all you know,' I said;
'The register of sentient things is dead.'
With only Ego left, in drastic coup,
I then pronounced the pronoun 'I' taboo.
The 'I,' the template of his empathy,
I twisted to a shapeless apathy!
No more his heart shall cast, as in a mold,

The hopes of God and mankind manifold.
I left him thus: with nothing more to write,
Composing madly, clever, never bright.
Without the 'I,' there is no 'You,' no 'They;'
So write; the world runs off the other way!
  "Now I, I, I, and you, my Muses Four,
To shake this mood shall undertake a tour.
By bloody curses, need I be more blunt,
I must address my troops on every front:
The more we do, the more we must get done!
Those gen'rals who win battles one on one
Are worth their salts, and privates worth their peppers,
Who are like us such Liberated steppers!
So don your denims, girls, and burn your bras,
The wizard I've become of women's wars!
Dismiss at once, along with bird and bee,
Monopolies with men on top of me!
Good Smugness, is that done? How super fine!
Now place their weapons in this palm of mine.
All ladies must, in matters so complex,
Aggress like angry men to claim their sex.
If any sense a contradiction here,
Just tell the bull: Go contemplate the steer!
Anality, my dear, confirm my cause;
Self-Service, please, a kiss with your applause;

Fair Sadism, stand aside, a smile will do;
For later pleasures, put away that shoe!
We've picked a perfect moment not to wait,
Attila and the Hun have left the gate;
The need for brawny men in metal shirts
To keep those rapists from our rusty skirts
Is past, along with muskets, bows and such:
Push-button war demands a woman's touch!"†

    How geometrically times have changed;
Divinities themselves become deranged:
Where once our Goddess drew a quiet breath
And simply bored the world to silent death,
Today with help from Dewey, Marx and Freud,
Her Nature bares a vengeance unalloyed.
Her ancient mother Night was once content
With father Chaos when their day was spent,
To let the Greek and Roman Empires go
With nothing but the usual godly show.
They'd stand aghast to see their daughter plow
The fields of other gods in name of NOW,††
To do Diana's thing for Women's Rights,
And doom them out of hand by all her lights;
To do her awful best in each arena,
Where *polis*††† once enjoyed that peach Athena.
We mortals shouldn't be surprised at all

---

†Prior to the 'modern era,' cultural norms—construction, farming, war—were founded upon the superior strength of the male forearm. Woman's passive and 'secondary' role followed from this. The minimization of the male forearm by an impersonal industrial and military technology places a premium on mental as opposed to physical prowess and renders the sexes equally effective within the culture.
††National Organization for Women.
†††*Polis:* Government, politics, society (Gr.).

To find her fleshing out where others fall.
When other gods depart, you may be sure,
Great Dullness by her Nature will endure.
Once Heaven's emptied by the hand of man,
We'll greet her forbears where it all began.
Just as the ear at birth is first to form,
Her stress on noise becomes an infant's norm;
The West declines in sound, as Spengler said,
And finds it best to listen once it's dead:
In death, the ear is also last to go,
And rings beyond the point where sense would know;
So Dullness in our name will boast of Night,
When none on earth at last recalls the Light!
    That skeptic Pope perhaps would be astounded
To find how all his broadsides had rebounded,
And that, despite the heavy bombing he had done,
This ancient target needs a brand-new gun:
From olden times to ours, this bumptious Queen
Has grown much more obnoxious in between;
Where once she used her pertness and her pout,
She marches now and lets it all hang out!
The few who read him go so far to say
That, in presumption, Pope became her prey,
To think that he of all mankind alone,
Could stop that mighty brain through all that bone;

Indeed, our Goddess seems immune to harm,
And packs on added poundage with each bomb!
In any case, her boundaries exceed by far
The frailties of Pope's and Queen Anne's War.†
As man fans forward in his strange parade,
We find her plastic banners bright arrayed;
Though Gardist poets are her darlings still,
Their empty doings leave her time to kill:
In every human effort, as you name it,
Where worthy impulse might arise, she'll tame it;
Where Grossness needs a prophet or a messenger,
You'll find her busier than Henry Kissinger.
As we shall see upon the day arising,
She still ascends by way of our devising!
   "By Jove, by mother Night and Chaos father,
How full the present brims from early bother!"
She had resumed. "Just look at all I've gained,
Now that I take up slack where others waned!
Old Plato thought that changes up in Heaven
Bred cultures here on earth that worked as leaven;
I've altered this, and through corruption here,
By special feedback, wreck the cosmic sphere!
See how I hang 'success' before their souls,
These asses, as the wagon 'progress' rolls;
How high they pile their wealth against their death,

---

†Queen Anne reigned during part of Pope's life (1702-1714).

Which blows it all away with every breath;
How far I drag them through their profit curves
Before remitting what such sloth deserves.
A case in point? Incorporated sham
That burnt to primal ash all Viet Nam
And shattered millions like a shrug from Hell:
As profits rose, great, priceless cultures fell!
How I, the prophet of your favored brands,
Exude a loathsome cancer from my glands,
Kill species with this poison from my pores,
Then call the profits 'theirs,' the ruin 'yours.'
These banks are trimmer than the British Fleet,
You see, to keep an Empire clean and neat!
O yes, believe me, with my handy whip,
I skyward drive your Comsat† from my hip
To every continent where I am able
To clean a country out and leave my label!
Free Enterprise, complete with total myth,
I press between the leaves of Adam Smith;
And, as for Liberties that men dispose,

---

†The U.S. spent ten years and tens of billions of tax dollars developing the technology for a satellite communications system and then through Comsat, a pseudo-public corporation, handed over major components of it to several large corporations, among them Western Union, Fairchild and RCA. This system eventually will generate control over all communications, both domestic and international, from 'Dial-A-Joke,' and *I Love Lucy* to 'CandyGrams.' It will tie the world in a knot by way of lasers, satellites and earth stations.

What man forfends what banks would feign foreclose?"†
  Such deadly contradictions Dullness wrought
To cancel out our epoch with her ought,
Compound our expectation and its heroes
By all her empty and inflated zeroes.
Where is that Eden Deists prophesied
Would make America on every side
A New Jerusalem to tame and bless
The Tiger Evil in a Wilderness?
The Urbi, Orbi Zeno once extolled
As by the stoa with the Greeks he strolled;
The Word that from the throat of Logos came
To give to *civitas* a Golden†† name;
The shaft of light by Egypt's Atheneum,
The bolt of blue above Rome's Coliseum,
That lit both minaret and Christian stable
And blazed upon the Grail at Arthur's table;
That brought what interregnum men had found
In Commonality to common ground?
Where has that Fundamental Justice gone
That broke like thunder on the prophet's tongue
To warn that emnities like flesh decay
To Elemental Oneness in a day?
  The Brotherhood such tendencies bespoke
Is with Primeval Forests lost in smoke;

---

†When the City of New York defaulted, the banks gave up the guise of working behind the scenes and moved out front to sit in on City Council meetings, disposing of virtually all its fiscal business by unchallenged decree. They continue to do so (1977), violating both the letter and spirit of the U.S. Constitution, the Constitution of the State of New York, the rights of the City Government and the general public.
††*Civatas*, or citizenship, may be said to have assumed a Golden name during the Golden Age of Pericles.

The furnaces of Empire rage and fume
And shunt our Birthright up a wanton flume:
Americans are asked to contemplate
The massive workings of a modern state,
The fiscal meshings of atomic nations,
With strictly Mercantilist calculations:
Good God! Free Enterprise and laissez-faire
Rocked off with Whitney† and his wicker chair!
How can we feed these big-time atom breeders††
The kind of corn we bagged for chicken feeders?
The 'carny' cry: "Behold supply, demand!"
Just means the eye still lags behind the hand,
Too slow to catch a thumb at second deal,
Or logic fixed upon a weighted wheel!
    But even as we take one dragon's head,
The Goddess spawns a thousand in its stead.
"So much for that," her Dullness then had stated;
"This stay among my forces finds me sated."
But, like familiars of a noted sot,
Her Muses knew the pitfalls of her lot;
Like every drunk who always needs one more,
Her Present sprawled upon the Future's floor;
The thrust of all the Goddess saw and heard
Lay in corruption of the Written Word;
For being Greek she needs no other brief:

---

†Eli Whitney (1765-1825).
††Breeder reactors produce as a by-product plutonium, the key element in the
international rage for nuclear weapons.

All Form is webbed within the Poet's leaf;
Society, to fail in every part,
Must wither first within the Poet's heart!
Now this she had achieved to some degree,
Else how account for what we are, and see?
The trouble is, with all this poetry stuff,
She never knew when she had had enough:
She gave the painter-poets† total sway
With empty sense impression, 'till today
Poetic Realms make simple mortals wince
So much that only Rod†† will sit as Prince;
And when you thought that verse could get no worse,
She named Diane Wakoski Royal Nurse;
Since this was Bedlam, just to make it more so,
She gave the cap to Koch, the bells to Corso;†††
Now that she had the Castle really whirlin',
She called in Willie Merwin as her Merlin!
Once in the pan, to sop his Muse's ire,
McCarthy†††† tossed the Kingdom in the fire!
Before the fat became too drawn and lean,
She named Diane DiPrima Virgin Queen,
Who put the whole thing out by blowin' cool:
And so today we have the Modern School
Of poets bloody, bold and sinister
And dumb! Shapiro as Prime Minister!†††††

---

†That sub-school of Existential Poetry, which holds that poetry should strive
for the impersonal effects of non-representational art, a patent impossibility,
since words are by their absolute nature representational.
††Rod McKuen, of course.
†††Both Kenneth Koch and Gregory Corso attempt wit in their verse.
††††Former Senator Eugene McCarthy, the politician and poet, in that order.
†††††Karl Shapiro is a great exponent of poetry devoid of all apparent form,
ostensibly to throw off the shackles of Europe and get right down to the true
American thing, whatever that is.

BOOK THE SECOND

Argument

The Goddess within her Computerized Bunker. Through her Manipulations here, She reduces the World of Letters to her Ends of Chaos and Darkness. Her Toast to all the Poets of the Realm. Her Fear that some Renegade Bard might confound her Work. She perceives a Need for a Laureate to bind her Legions into a Vanguard of Banality. Her Strategy: to make her Laureate so Prominent that Reality will not intrude within her Kingdom, thus assuring its Ultimate Destruction.

She's still abroad, this strange and giddy Queen,
To pack her Grossness with no space between:
Hard by "The Y," at Ninety-two and Lex.,
She feeds computers her most potent hex!
From there, at console banks, most vast and various,
She prints-out syllabi, so daft yet serious,
To keep our verse so bad, so bound to bore,
That few, we know, can stand it anymore!
She need but throw a switch, then give a wiggle,
To make a million little letters jiggle!
No, never had the Goddess such a power
To realize Ambition as this hour
Within her cozy, bunker-like abode
Reduce a Continent to Saturn's lode,†
By rhapsodizing on old Wiener's†† curse,
An organ with a clef from bad to worse,
Until all Excellence depart the air
And only nonsense reach the dullard ear,
And, by her automated fingertips,
All poets die or speak with dummy lips!
   From this electron-generated bowel,
She drapes with awful moss remote MacDowell,
Dooms bards at Ossabaw to swamps and crocs'
And Yaddo††† hopes to Gibsons on the rocks!
By turning 'Standards' to position 'Off,'

---

†In the chemical language of Pope's time, Saturn was lead. See *The Dunciad*,
line 28.
††Norbert Wiener, known as the "father" of electronic computers.
†††MacDowell, Ossabaw and Yaddo are, of course, all artists' colonies.

She brings banality, embossed, from Knopf!
Like Hacker† bound in rich, ornate edition,
To verify the NBA condition,
That verse, as poison, should be relegated;
If poor enough, then only, elevated,
By judges, experts on the dirty novel,
Who never knew this dame from Andrew Marvell!
 Ah, this switch here! She turns a headless screw in,
Now Random House has *two*, not *one* McKuen;
This sorts the poetry bin at Doubleday††
And gives the cleaning woman final say!
That 'Confrontation' toggle, watch the sparks!
Drives disenfranchised poets back to Marx,
To swallow whole their causes and espouse
The country's downfall in a coffee-house!
 This clump of tangled, disconnected loops
Connects to Blacks and other ethnic groups,
And makes James Weldon Johnson's native bones
Dance mumbo-jumbo with Baraka-Jones!
The Women Poets' switch, marked 'Super Gall,'
Means One Minority outnumbers All,
That any pampered, ranting wrathful bitch
Is hailed the latest Sexton, Plath or Rich!
This circuit will make sure that Academia
Avoids all fare that might enrouge anemia,

---

†Marilyn Hacker received the National Book Award for Poetry in 1975. The next year, Alfred A. Knopf gave a fine edition to her next book, *Separations*, which was even worse than the first.
††I have never met anyone at any publishing house who made a claim to knowing how to select poetry, so I have surmised that it's being done by anyone who has nothing else to do.

Keeps thin all forms, makes substance only *seem*,
The notion of Narcissus on a stream,
A wan, reflected face, a rippling gloss,
Bewitching *The New Yorker's* Howard Moss!†
   This switch will banish rage to City Lights,
To San Francisco wharfs and hobo nights,
So any bardic function it performs
Will never penetrate prevailing norms!
Just push that button marked 'Bob Bly's "Deep" thing,'††
St. Olaf's Chapel gets a brand-new wing;
This switch sends Dickey in a glass canoe
Up river as a Roebuck Phil Freneau;
The 'Kenyon' switch, behaving downright foreign,
Traps Rabbit Ransom in his Brooks and Warren;
The 'Brinnin'††† button, past its better days,
Dispatches books on boats down slipp'ry ways;
'Ashbery, John,' a switch to be the rage,
Short of its goal, the poem as empty page!
   Once Smugness crossed some wires, the little fool!
And turned out Breadloafs at Black Mountain School!††††
The Goddess was so miffed, that just for spite,
She taught two Princesses at Bard to write!
That circuit there, with just a little boost,

---

†Howard Moss as poetry editor of *The New Yorker* has played a key role in keeping Existential poets before the public eye, to the exclusion of any other kind unless they are well known enough to pull their weight in ads.
††Bly has a theory about 'deep metaphors,' which are supposed to tap subconscious forces. St. Olaf's is a small Protestant college in Minnesota, where Bly began writing poetry in 1946 before moving on to Harvard.
†††Malcolm Brinnin wrote a book on ocean liners.
††††Breadloaf and Black Mountain hold conferences for writers, propounding opposing views of poetry.

Can jolt Naropa's Rocky Mountain roost,†
Where Ginsberg, hair and "Howl" a little thinner,
By Buddhist bells chants 'Om' for curry dinner,
While Burroughs, Sanders, Waldman,†† at the feast,
Then tax, in turns, the Wisdom of the East,
And ask the ghost of Williams††† to the site,
To see such ign'rant Swamis clash by night!
    This toggle here, by Ma Bell's space-bound trolleys,
Conveys Yale's Younger Poets' Oldster Follies,
Where Crusty Mountain and her Scholar Spouse
Urge forth their smallish, mostly annual Mouse!
She keeps the Hotline clear to Harvard Yard
To help Ciardi†††† coach each bulging bard
On how to butter up his daily dozens
To please the Grandma taste of Norman Cousins;†††††
And lest a major poet show his nose,
She maintained Robert Lowell in the pose,
Who had, should lectures falter, Muses fret,
Ex-wife Elizabeth's elite gazette!††††††
    This red switch here, still hot from too much use,
Sets pirates of the Banks and Business loose
To plunder Publishing's abject estates
In search of fronts for their Conglomerates:
Now Random House plays foil for RCA,
And Holt, facade for CBS this way;

---

†The Naropa Institute in Boulder, Colo., is one of those Buddhist centers stressing poetry now cropping up in different sections of the country.
††William Burroughs, Ed Sanders, Anne Waldman all seem to teach and meditate at this place (1976-77).
†††William Carlos Williams, Ginsberg's avowed mentor.
††††John Ciardi.
†††††Norman Cousins' *Saturday Review* always favored Ciardi and his ilk.
††††††Elizabeth Hardwick is a 'power' at *New York Review of Books*, which of course helped. The Lowells, with Jason and Barbara Epstein, were the founders of NYRB.

Bobbs-Merrill, now IT and T's new toy,
An imprint Chile's Colonels might enjoy,
Which will, at least until the uproar stops,
Print only Picture Books for tabletops,
And give, for now, its editors *carte blanche:*
Who kills the root need never cut the branch,
But leave the foliage its usual face
To blow dumbfounded through the Marketplace!
But what of Language, Paine's and Zenger's trust,
Of Books, those gatherers of golden dust,
That once to hold was then to feel and see
That what was truly made has made men free?†
Has set Walt Whitman's theme to wane and wax
And ring within the mind like Bunyan's ax;
Kept deep and cool the conscience of Thoreau,
And rattled skeptics with the pen of Poe,
And let the Native Spirit walk or run
To catch a little light with Emerson?
   So walk or run, just pull that lever there
And plunge Great Expectations to despair
As Little Presses start their anxious runs
To pop the Big Shots with their stapling guns:
They all turn into Blakes and Horace Greeleys,
Concocting stranger stuff than Huxley's 'Feelies';††
Their poems, when poured for tonnage, are Concrete,

---

†The 'Ascent of Man' depends upon his devotion to his skills. A. J. Bronowski, a paraphrase.
††In *Brave New World,* one of Huxley's contemplated new forms of synthesized experience was the 'feelie,' which when held and rubbed, provoked sexual arousal.

Yet hit and run like fog on skittish feet;†
The Females tear the shroud by Sappho woven
To bloody shreds and ribbons for their coven,
And then employ with Jong her verbal blender
To prove that crap can come from any gender!
There go the tankas, haikus, quickee! Lookie!
They've harnessed Einstein in a Fortune Cookie!
See Dullness now become Mercutio's Mab,
Although a little stoned from sipping Tab:
She's moved so many presses underground,
That vacancies above now quite abound,
And Alternate Composers cough such phlegm,
The world awaits Alternatives to them!
    At last, the lever of the Federal Fount,
The NEA, †† which has by recent count,
For every poet that it placed in schools,†††
Put two politicos on Public Rolls!
O, what a strange melange of little wires!
That spark these hard and gem-like muffled fires
In mountains, mudflats, ghettoes and *barrios*
Up by the Harlem! And down by the *rios!*
As Citizens, so poor and so bereft,
That only Sex and Age and Race are left,
Who are not counted poets when alone,
But once amassed as groups become so known,

---

†'skittish feet' of course suggests Sandburg's poem about fog.
††The National Endowment for the Arts.
†††The N.E.A. pays practicing poets to teach poetry in the primary and secondary schools.

Who, having missed their grants by other *schema*,
Now organize and grind out *terza rima*:
The Goddess and Len Randolph† have the sockets
For all of Deprivation's po'try pockets!
No application form is ever tabled,
So long as social stigma can be labeled:
We now have hosts of Reservation Okies
Conversant with the terms of broken trochees;
And, equally piquant, some oldster nuns,
Now funded to compose their Donne-like puns,
And many pre-school children can be found
Who dash off unrhymed cantos after Pound!
    O, Paradise, most palpable on earth!
Where else could Dullness place and plump her girth
With such a sense of Presence unconfined
As in the pillowed bureaucratic mind!
Which in the name of democratic rules
Confuses poets with the hustler-ghouls,
And sidesteps charges of elitist cant
By fusing basal meanness to its grant!
Where else but on some Literature Board††
Could Dullness get her gravy train insured,
And bid Bill Phillips form CCLM,†††
To serve as her Petronius pro-tem,
Who, as an instance of the thing to do,

---

†Leonard Randolph is head of the Literature Program for the N.E.A.
††The N.E.A.'s Literature Panel allocates money.
†††C.C.L.M. is the Coordinating Council of Literary Magazines. The Government asked Phillips to oversee the formation of this private agency to supplement the granting function of the N.E.A. Literature Panel. While Phillips was a member of the C.C.L.M., many times the chairman, this body voted tens-of-thousands of dollars to the *Partisan Review*, which he edits.

Confers a windfall on his own Review!†
   "Behold them all! Then raise a royal toast
To idiots who flaunt their monarch's boast!"
The Goddess called: "My Chaos is complete,
And drives the Darkness by degrees replete
With nuclear catastrophes impending,
To blow my Empire into Night unending!"
As Rommel with a sniff of distant Nile,
And Patton at the Elbe both paused awhile,
To plumb that peak from which their panting will
Knew progress henceforth would be all downhill,
She mused and let the moment fizz!
Then called her helpmates for their daily quiz:
"Who sings 'Go Forward' when she sends you back?"
She urged. "Who's up is *where*? Whose red is *black*?
Whose foot is smaller than the tightest inch?
Who topples backward at the slightest pinch?
Put down those hands! I haven't finished yet!
Anality, go get the plums, my pet!
We'll hold a crazy party and a quiz combined
To plunge us into normal frames of mind!
Now, Smugness, that is *not* a *normal* smile!
Stout Sadism, slap that ingrate for a while!
Self-Service fetch the whips but don't be long!
We still have lashes if you answer wrong!

---

†The same *Partisan Review*, of course.

All right? Get set! Get ready, now, and go:
Whose first priorities are wrong we know?
Who eats the margarine and calls it butter?
Who, when on skates or skis, can be so utter?
Whose metric ton converts to Celsius ounce?
And last, who keeps it special for the Dunce?
Now if you know the answer, step aside!
The first to shout it out, I'll have her hide!
The last to tell it, too, will get it double!
So come to think of it, you're all in trouble!
Now, Sadism, see that justice here is done
And give them all the nine-tails, one by one!"
     Such sessions drove her up arousal's wall,
To dizzy heights where even Eve might fall,
Beyond the peak where Porter† lost the tune,
Then bumped her back to earth, but none too soon!
Her scheme seemed perfect! Triumph all but certain!
"But what," she thought, "should Chance derail my curtain?
Should unknown poets come as ten Nerudas
To swallow up my bards like barracudas,
And reassert the poets' savage right
As arbiter of Ends and Moral Might,
That I've bootlegged to Science in my time,
And overwhelm me with their awful rhyme!"
Like Faustus, in obsession, or Macbeth,

---

†Cole Porter.

She needed final proof, or further death,
Some massive weight upon the crooked pan,
Lest hidden justice countervail her plan!
She thought and thought about it, long and deep;
She took it out; she laid it down to sleep,
Until at last she told the tattered four:
"I need a Cibber as I had before!
I'm never old! Besides, through exercise,
I still can pack a cannon up my thighs!
I need a poet who will trim my crown
With epic trifles of my last renown!
Who'll swell to mighty realms on many pages
The bubble rainbows of my final stages!
Whose sense of human purpose coils so small
It cannot raise the roof where passions crawl!
Who'll screw the scope of Ethics to the glass
So close that only petty scruples pass:
Through him, they might eclipse that cosmic host
Of Common Terrors that persuade the ghost
Of Death to lie with Eros in the bone
And never dare to mate with me alone!
O, witty consort! Existential liege!
Whose bubble poems outbounce potential siege!
Whose playful punk upon polluted air
Throws perfume to obscure my presence there!

Who'll help replace the impulse of poesis
With Teller's† deadly Scientistic thesis,
As Dionysian forces then conspire
To overload deep motives with their fire,
Until the Earth that man no longer knows
Explodes, as still the bubble poet blows!
    "In short, a Cibber now I need at once
To serve as both my Laureate and Dunce!
But, O, to choose!" she moaned. "They're all so bad!
The vice of one, like clap, has lept from pad to pad:
They each, with packaged seed, on Olson's†† ground,
By rote implant their out-of-season Pound;
Or pray the Eliotic bulb, that hot-house ward,
Will blossom forth without the help of God;
That Beckett's wide effects might be achieved
Without destruction of the Faith believed;
That they might glimpse the light of Stevens' star
By simply tinting blue an old guitar!
Who do not know that poems which catch the breath
Can breathe themselves because they grapple death,
And thrive on perils of the pruning-knife
That glances close against the throat of life!"

---

†Edward Teller became the arch-advocate of producing the bigger and bigger bomb, playing, at least in this sense, Cain to Oppenheimer's Abel.
††Charles Olson posited 'projectivist' verse, which was to be composed according to 'field.'

BOOK THE THIRD

Argument

The Manner in which the Goddess chooses her Laureate. The dire Straits of his Sojourn in Paris. His Preoccupation with Mirrors. The Mirror shatters, and with it the Poet's Identity and his Enslavement to the Ideal of non-verbal Poems. He destroys his Books, free at last. The Goddess arrives in Paris, restores the Mirror and rescues the Poet. She whisks him to New York, where he is feted and ordained as her King and Laureate.

Since verse by one could bear the other's name,
And all were interchangeably the same,
She simply started with the letter "A"
And asked the alphabet to lead the way.
Then with a finger as a dousing-fork,
She down the girded "A" 's just let it walk;
From 'Aiken,' 'Amis,' 'Ammons,' it went on,
Until it reached the name 'Ashbery, John'!
That name, however she might push or shove,
Was like a magnet to the joint above,
And wouldn't let her move it up or down,
Until she pledged 'Ashbery, John' the crown!
How right she was to let the Fates prevail:
A Harvard Grad who won a Prize at Yale!†
Who felt that Verse so badly failed the age
Because it had not put the sound of Cage,††
With all the force of calligraphs by Kline,†††
Enjoined with Beckett's analogic line,
Into a kind of Audenesque address,
That doubles back with Stevens-like†††† finesse,

---

†Ashbery won the Yale Younger Poets Award in 1955.
††John Cage, the experimental composer, had a profound influence, we are told, upon the poet. Ashbery has spoken of his first encounter with Cage's work following a two-year period during which he was unable to write: "I was jolted out of this by going with Frank O'Hara—I think it was New Year's Day, 1952—to a concert of . . . John Cage's 'Music of Changes.' It was a series of dissonant chords, mostly loud with irregular rhythms. It went on for over an hour and seemed infinitely extendable. I felt profoundly refreshed after listening to that. I started to write again shortly afterwards. I felt that I could be as singular in my art as Cage was in his." *The N.Y. Times Sunday Magazine*, May 23, 1976.
†††Franz Kline, the modern painter who dealt with bold calligraphic forms.
††††Ashbery has called Wallace Stevens "my favorite poet."

And by a subtle overlay of optics,†
Is shattered as the shuttered gaze of Coptics,
To give our age a dazzling sense of Self
That might compete with Prufrock on the shelf!
"Now this," he told O'Hara, "we should do,
If for no other reason than it's new!
Then once its done, the future could be spent
In asking people what we really meant!"
    Through his unique investiture by Dullness,
John soon would bring this all to utter fullness,
By using words as either hue or note
To *seem* or *sound* but never quite *denote*,
Which like an inmate with a damaged mind,
May wander wildly yet remain confined,
And maunder through the wards of modern art,
While Dullness counts the cash in Plato's mart!
'Ashbery, John's' ambitions from the first
Seemed in their sense of present time accursed:
He wondered how to get the world to wait
Just long enough to bring him up to date,
And still prevent, by moving on so fast,
The future from decaying to the past!
Or how the recent poet had persisted
When Modern Verse 'till him had not existed?††
He floated far upon the Crimson Tide†††

---

†Ashbery says that a major influence in his life was his maternal grandfather, Henry Lawrence, a physics professor. Ashbery's poems all involve the way the mind can alter perception as a prism might alter the aspect of an object, by virtue of a change in its own position or the amount of light passing through it.
††Speaking of the early 1950s, Ashbery has said: "We were all young and ambitious then. American painting seemed the most exciting art around. American poetry was very traditional at that time, and there was no modern poetry in the sense that there was modern painting."
†††Harvard, of course, is also sometimes known as the Crimson Tide.

With waterwings like these against his side,
Where premises, sophistic'ly adept,
Like Carter's promises, need not be kept;
Where all a friendship with O'Hara† garners
Is frittered quite away in Auden Honors;††
And even Yale's Award had lost its luster†††
In light of other names within its muster!
So when the Goddess chose him at that hour,
He stood in shadow by Our Lady's†††† tower,
And couldn't see his own impending reign,
But only sunset sinking in the Seine!
For ever since he first arrived in France,
His shadow had been tutor to mischance:
He heavily had shed Manhattan air,
Because, he said, the present wasn't there;
Yet once in France, and travel as he might,
The morning aged to noon, noon grew to night;
And, in what often seemed the final wrench,
He found that all of France spoke only French;†††††
While in the States, the critics through misprise,
Reduced to kindling-wood his sapling "Trees!"††††††

---

†Ashbery first met O'Hara at Harvard.
††Ashbery did his honors thesis at Harvard on Auden. Also, Auden as the sole judge for the Yale award in 1955, gave the prize to Ashbery's poems, so our Laureate was off and running, though he still complains it was an unpromising start.
†††The Yale Series of Younger Poets has come up with a remarkable number of dud-recipients both before and after Ashbery.
††††Notre Dame. Ashbery spent ten years in Paris (1956-66).
†††††When he first arrived in France, he says, he felt "lonely and deprived of American talk. I could not yet speak French and therefore didn't hear people on the street say things that would move me."
††††††His first professionally published volume was *Some Trees* (1956).

O, see him then, so goaded by these tongues
To lend a foreign verb his New York lungs;
A dot along the quay engulfed in fog,
Ingesting his remorse like Zola's frog;†
Who buys an English book for teenage boys††
To lend his alchemy some new alloys,
And make him sick for where he's never been,
Like Auden's limestone hills††† in Nineteen-ten.
Below the eaves, above the *abattoir*,
He tries for mixtures never hit before,
By using paragraphs from *Esquire*†††† mags,
The ashes of Gitanes, which he calls 'fags,'
Combined with Webern's††††† notes and Magritte's paint,
To shape a poem devoid of verbal taint!††††††
When all at once, while looking in the glass,

---

†Zola once said that he, like everyone else, had to swallow his 'toad of remorse' when he got up in the morning.

††We have already mentioned Ashbery's confiscation of passages from a British children's book, *Beryl of the Biplane*, by William LeQueux. One source for the later *Rivers and Mountains* (1966), Ashbery says, was *Three Hundred Things a Bright Boy Can Do* (England, 1911).

†††Referring to Auden's poem about such 'limestone hills.'

††††*Esquire* mags. Describing the composition of "Europe" (1960), Ashbery is quoted as saying: "I remember writing it in a state of confusion about what I wanted to do . . . I'd get American magazines like *Esquire*, open the pages, get a phrase from it, and then start writing on my own. When I ran out, I'd go back to the magazine."

†††††Composer Anton Webern. Ashbery has said: "I also got the idea from Anton Webern to isolate a particular word, as you would isolate a particular note to feel it in a new way."

††††††The reviewer Richard Kostelanetz has written of Ashbery (Sunday *Times*, May 23, 1976): "The more one talks with Ashbery the clearer it becomes the principal inspirations for his poems are other books and then works of music or, occasionally, of visual art. The experiences of his non-cultural life scarcely appear in his poetry." Ashbery is throughout irrationally offended by the characteristics of language, its need for syntax, association, coherent recall, in other words, by its very nature. So perhaps he should have tried painting (we may suspect he has), which has always seemed to interest him more.

The mirror† summoned him: "Attend, you ass!
Too much self-scrutiny," it slowly spoke,
"Is still bad luck, you know!" And then it broke!
The glass, in shattered sections, with its sheen,
Fell with the keenness of a guillotine,
And severed, with a crunch upon the floor,
The imaged head that it had held before;
As surely as a blade against the neck,
It slew that poet in that crystal wreck!
    The poet dead, the man rejoined the hand,††
And then rejoiced to reassume command
Of lips and nose, the mustache clipped so well,
The treasured parts reserved for 'Show and Tell':
Now all lept forth, like natives to the touch,
And broke the grip of old Mephisto's clutch,
Escaped the terms whereby, through Faustian dole,
John swapped his body for a 'poet's soul';†††

---

†All Existential poets, and off-hand we may include here Brinnin, Merrill, Moss, Merwin and Strand, among others, have a peculiar proclivity for reflected vistas which usually feature themselves at the center. This may be a lake or wading pool, but more often than not it is simply a mirror.
††Ashbery quotes, unless otherwise specified, are from *Self-Portrait in a Convex Mirror*, The Penguin Poets, 1976.

"... This severed hand
Stands for life, and wander as it will,
East or West, north or south, it is ever
A stranger who walks beside me."

—from "Worsening Situation," p. 3.

†††John is eminently conscious of the subtler ramifications of his strange mission to forge poetic analogies to developments in painting and music. But is he aware of the more obvious fact that in his own life he has reversed Faust's exchange with Mephistopheles? Faust gave up his soul for things of this world and the flesh. Ashbery, on the other hand, has edited from his poems almost all direct experience of the flesh in this world, to isolate and purify the abstract, formal, or merely esthetic aspects of 'reality'; or, in other words, to gain a 'poet's soul.'

Contracted for the poem as picture deal;†
And appetite for form made sense unreal,
Until the substance of his art became
Much less important than the picture's frame;
And John himself, and all his world, alas,
Quite cold and frozen in that chosen glass!††
        No longer poet now, but man of men,
Like 'instant mystics,' he was 'born again'!†††

---

†As stated, painting was, and still appears to be, Ashbery's central interest. As a youth, he attended the Museum School in Rochester. In his adult life, most of his writing has been about art, for the Paris *Herald Tribune* and, from 1965-72, for *Art News*. The major guiding and informing figures in his life all seem to have been painters. He labors almost obsessively to exclude all moral, philosophical and even emotional elements from his poetry, to deal with changing surfaces within a representational void, like the Abstract Expressionist painters. His struggle to develop, expand and sustain his work, to paint, as it were, with a writer's equipment of language, like the effort of a moth to penetrate a lightbulb, cannot be really appreciated without keeping such considerations uppermost in mind.

††His theory has varnished him into the surface of things:

"The glass chose to reflect only what he saw
Which was enough for his purpose: his image
Glazed, embalmed . . .

"That the soul is a captive, treated humanely, kept
In suspension, unable to advance much further . . .

"And just as there are no words for the surface, that is,
No words to say what it really is, that it is not
Superficial but a visible core, then there is
No way out of the problem of pathos vs. experience.
You will stay on, restive, serene in
Your gesture which is neither embrace nor warning
But which holds something of both in pure
Affirmation that doesn't affirm anything."
                    —from "Self-Portrait in a Convex Mirror," pp. 68-70.

†††It is perhaps already necessary to explain that America in the 70s was obsessed with being 'born again.' This is the subject of many current books and of, doubtless, more to come.

Not as reflected, simply as he was,
A child of purpose in a world with cause:
The necrophilic manner he had bred
To lend his lines the 'rigors' of the dead;†
Those triple negatives and cracked dissolves,††

---

†Ashbery's world weariness, expression of *ennui* and *deja vu* make Eliot appear a civic booster by comparison:

"But I was trying to tell you about a strange thing
That happened to me, but this is no way to tell about it,
By making it truly happen. It drifts away in fragments.
And one is left sitting in the yard
To try to write poetry
Using what Wyatt and Surrey left around,
Took up and put down again
Like so much gorgeous raw material,
As though it would always happen in some way
And meanwhile since we are all advancing
It is sure to come about in spite of everything
On a Sunday, where you are left sitting
In the shade that, as always, is just a little too cool."
                                        —from "Grand Galop," p. 19.

This is the dominant—well, 'thrust' is too strong a word—*ambience*, perhaps.

††Ashbery's multiple negatives, like black holes in the cosmos, suck the mind to nowhere and beyond:

"Focus in the tragic melancholy of the bright stare
Into nowhere, a hole like the black holes in space."
                                        —from "Forties Flick," p. 5.

"Yes, but—there are no 'yes, buts,'
The body is what this is all about and it disperses
In sheeted fragments, all somewhere around
But difficult to read correctly since there is
No common vantage point, no point of view
Like the 'I' in a novel. And in truth
No one *never* saw the *point of any* . . ." (Italics added)
                                        —from "No Way of Knowing," p. 56.

The contradictions of his own resolves;†
The fractured aspect of Abstract cachet;
The foppish languors of Laforgue's sachet††
The forced, remote disjunctions††† in his poems,
That brought the strangest traffic to his rooms:

---

†Positive assertions in Ashbery are invariably set forth to serve as premises for
vetoes or filibusters:

"Or, to take another example: last month
I vowed to write more. What is writing?
Well, in my case, it's getting down on paper
Not thoughts, exactly, but ideas, maybe:
Ideas about thoughts. Thought is too grand a word.
Ideas is better, though not precisely what I mean.
Someday I'll explain. Not today though."
                              —from "Ode to Bill," p. 50.

††Where Eliot restricted Laforgue's voice to Prufrock, let us say, Ashbery seems
to have confiscated it as an integral persona.
†††'remote disjunctions':

"Ask a hog what is happening. Go on. Ask him.
The road just seems to vanish
And not that far in the distance, either. The horizon must have
    been moved up."
                              —from "Grand Galop," p. 20.

"These trains, people, beaches, rides
In happiness because their variety
Is outlived but still there, outside somewhere,
In the side yard, maybe."
                              —from "Poem in Three Parts," p. 23.

"And the air pours in with piano notes
In its skirts, as though to say, 'Look, John,
I've brought these and these'—that is,
A few Beethovens, some Brahmses, . . .'"
                              —from "Fear of Death," p. 49.

A mountain in the sherbet dish,† you'd think,
Or subways running late along the sink!
That placed all *objects* in the deepest pain:††
Had parking-meters catching cold in rain,
The bank in love, the doughnut shop betrayed,
The hotel dying and the church dismayed!
And yet, for all this *schmaltz*, could not see fit
To feel one pang for *man*††† in all of it—

---

†'A mountain in the sherbet dish':

"Those sisters slink into the sapphire
Hair that is mounting day.
There are still other made-up countries
Where we can hide forever,
Wasted with eternal desire and sadness,
Sucking the *sherbets*, crooning the tunes, naming the names."

(Italics added)
—from "Hop O'My Thumb," p. 33.

†† *objects* in the deepest pain':

". . . what lethargy in the avenues . . ."

—from "As You Came from the Holy Land," p. 6.

"This painful freshness of each *thing* being exactly itself . . ."

(Italics added)
—from "Voyage in the Blue," p. 27.

"With the sky now a bit impatient for the day to be over
Like a bored salesgirl shifting from foot to stockinged foot."

—from "Grand Galop," p. 16.

"Better the months—
They are almost persons— . . ."

—from "Grand Galop," p. 15.

††† 'one pang for *man*':

Though he indulges great sympathy for things, objects and natural entities like the sky and seasons, Ashbery, like an imperious sovereign, dismisses out of hand any difficulties his fellow mortals might happen to confront:

"His case inspires interest
But little sympathy; it is smaller
Than it first appeared."

—from "A Man of Words," p. 8.

So aptly writ: "Such foolishness shall pass!"
As now it had all shattered with the glass!
   He found the world restored in every phase:
La place! La salle! L'espoir of Sodus† days!
The clouds, Elysian lambs, rolled forth in pairs;
Forchette met spoon, la table went with chairs!
Not Pippa, no! Not Cristo†† from the sea
So madly cried: "The world belongs to me!"
The morning-glories blazed, the curtains hushed,
The Chopin record played, the toilet flushed!
The use of each facility, he found,
Insisted on new philosophic ground,
For those who all the comforts would engage
Become perforce exponents of the age;
And sinks that work do more than Sartre can
To stopper-up the void that troubles man!†††
The noisy, dauntless autos *dans la rue*
Honked out: "*La vie en rose*, old John, pursue!"
More loudly than that lazy, dirty bird

---

†John was born in Sodus, a small town near Rochester, N.Y.
††The Count of Monte Cristo, of course, who after long imprisonment and final emergence from the sea, climbed to a rock and shouted: "The world is mine!" So John must have felt to be relieved of the awful burden of his contract with destiny to turn poetry into science, prose, painting or music:

"I feel as though someone had made me a vest
Which I was wearing out of doors into the countryside
Out of loyalty to the person, although
There is no one to see, except me
With my inner vision of what I look like.
The wearing is both a duty and pleasure
Because it absorbs me, absorbs me too much."
                                —from "Ode to Bill," p. 50.

†††It still seems remarkable that those cynics who so deplore the vacuity of all the usages of the modern age should be the first to over-indulge themselves in all its comforts and conveniences. John Ashbery is an outstanding case in point for this egregious, nay, almost overwhelming irony, as we shall see further.

Whose "jug-jug" once was in *The Waste Land* heard!
    He swept the pieces up as common trash,
And marveled that his death should leave no ash!
He never would write verse again at all.
But like his namesake† make a flaming pall
Of all he wrote and with a single stroke
Dispatch it as a plague in fire and smoke!
As Alice and Narcissus both had learned,
Who loves the mirror will at last be spurned;
Who studies his reflection as his soul
Must measure Heaven through a primate's hole;
Think Immortality is somehow found
In puppy love or poems or sterling pound;
Or mirrors with their monkey-like remove
Transcend our flesh and so then steadfast prove!
Parmigiano went quite mad, you see,
From trifling with the mirror's mercury,
To turn it to a solid man could hold
Much higher than the church's cross of gold.††

---

†In Pope's *Dunciad*, Colley Cibber suffered obscurity prior to being dubbed her 'Dunce' by Dullness.
††According to one account, Parmigiano, the central figure of Ashbery's "Self-Portrait in a Convex Mirror," gave up painting altogether (1537) to pursue alchemy. He found a mystic attraction in the mercury that served as the basis for the mirror's reflective capabilities. Somewhat like Ashbery, he felt the paths of science might lead more directly to spiritual absolutes. He worked feverishly in his makeshift lab to 'congeal' (or solidify) mercury. He staked both his sanity and his fortune on this fantastic venture. Finally, he was hounded to jail by his creditors. In a last desperate bid for survival, he turned back to his painting. But it was too late to recapture the powerful focus he once brought to his art and he died a broken and forgotten man (1540).
    Ashbery also is intrigued by what lies behind the looking-glass:

"Business is carried on by look, gesture,
Hearsay. It is another life to the city,
The backing of the looking glass of the
Unidentified but precisely sketched studio."

—from "Self-Portrait," p.75.

Now John, our poet-alchemist, whose pose
Would melt the poem to science, paint or prose,
Or more outlandishly than even that,
A kind of music without sharp or flat,†
Had now been spared that tragic spectacle:
The human heart as slaughtered hope's receptacle!

---

†His poems as science, paint, prose or music.
As science:

"But most of all she (the day) loved the particles
That transform objects of the same category
Into particular ones, each distinct
Within and apart from its own class."

—from "Scheherazade," p. 9.

As a painted picture:
    (The whole scheme of *Self-Portrait* bears this out.)

"News of something we know and care little of,
As the distant castle rejoices to the joyous
Sound of hooves, releasing rooks straight up into the faultless air
And meanwhile weighs its shadow ever heavier on the mirroring
Surface of the river, surrounding the little boat with three
    figures in it."

—from "Voyage in the Blue," p. 27.

As prose:
(Much of Ashbery's 'poetry' could be transferred to prose without mussing a comma. Sometimes he intends this to be the case, as in the following, where he quotes from life.)

"I really would like to know what it is you do to 'magnetize' your
poetry, where the curious reader, always a bit puzzled, comes
back for a clearer insight."

—from "The Tomb of Stuart Merrill," p. 38.

As music:
"What I like about music is its ability to be convincing, to carry an argument through successfully to the finish, though the terms of the argument remain unknown quantities. . . . I would like to do this in poetry." Ashbery made this statement in 1964.

"That is the tune but there are no words;
The words are only speculation
(From the Latin *speculum*, mirror)
They seek and cannot find the meaning of music."

—from "Self-Portrait," p. 69.

Destruction of the writer's books was next,
Which he acquired for title, not for text,†
For how their jackets might appoint the room,
Or tip his scribbler's cap with classic plume:
For weight of thought, his Toynbee hard to lift,
For wit and whimsy, noble, young Tom Swift!††
His Popular Mechanics,††† at a glance
Suggesting Leonardo's Renaissance!
Now this, for John, was joyous work indeed,
Who, by his poems, just doesn't like to read!
In any case, he tossed them on the grate;
And then *his* 'works,' all wrought at such a rate,
Those Scriptos, crammed with Frank O'Hara's tricks,††††

---

†'Not for text': "Here, as elsewhere, Ashbery freely acknowledges the sources of his poems, and even their titles, are frequently borrowed from others. As he explains, 'The title is a take-off point, a way of getting into the poem. It may not be the subject, but it is an aperture.' " From the *Times* interview with Kostelanetz.

††Tom Swift was to Ashbery's (and my own) generation what Horatio Alger was to the one before. With his fondness for juvenile literature, I can suppose that John still relishes Tom Swift's adventures with his motorcycle, flying machine and submarine, where mechanical know-how takes the place of moral rectitude as a major key to success.

†††Ashbery's most constant source of metaphors remains the sciences.

††††Perhaps no other person, outside of his immediate family and including his physicist grandfather, as noted, had a more profound influence on the poet than Frank O'Hara, who guided John toward atonal music, Abstract Expressionist art and his own New York School of verse. Ashbery makes great use of O'Hara's methods of composition, where the page is covered with associations that are then weeded down and refined for Pop or (in Ashbery's case) Op Art effects. Ashbery also is trained with O'Hara's eye to find iconographic effects in the most absolutely common-place utensils and occurrences, in lists of places visited, small chores accomplished, chit-chat, what was had for lunch, suggesting variety within monotony, exhaustion, dismay. This, from "Grand Galop," is typical of what Ashbery owes O'Hara:

"And today is Monday. Today's lunch is Spanish omelet, lettuce and
    Tomato salad,

Now with a rustle hit the fireplace bricks!
His oozing high school verse would lead the lot;
His *Trees*, † so utter Auden! *Turandot!*††
Those cryptic week-end††† epics he'd compose
By shuffling†††† up the lines of lifted prose;
Those unicorns conceived to bend the mind

Jello, milk and cookies. Tomorrow's: sloppy joe on bun,
Scalloped corn, stewed tomatoes, rice pudding and milk."

So we have Ashbery establishing his own poetic ground between Frank O'Hara's often brilliant humor on one side and Eliot's metaphysical ruminations on the other. Despite Ashbery's repeated citation of Auden, Stevens and W. C. Williams, among others, these two major influences continue to define his sensibility.

It should have been mentioned above that O'Hara's random compositional techniques paralleled those of Action Painters, like Pollock, etc.

---

†*Some Trees* (1956).
††*Turandot and Other Poems* (1953), Ashbery's first book, was published as a chapbook by John Bernard Myers, then director of the Tibor de Nagy Gallery. According to one account, a copy brought more than $500 on the rare book market (1977).
†††Ashbery still insists he does his 'serious writing' only on Saturday and Sunday: "I'm still a weekend poet," he told Kostelanetz. "It would be pointless to write poetry every day."
††††Speaking of a dry period, he told Kostelanetz, "It was time to shuffle the cards." The 'cards' turn out to be popular magazines, children's books, provocative 'classics' (Freud), all used ironically, which on one occasion resulted in "Europe" (1960), which Kostelanetz says is "one of the great long poems of recent years—a classic of coherent [sic!] diffuseness."
Here is the 52nd stanza in its entirety:

> "The rose
>   dirt
>   dirt you
> pay
> The buildings
>   is tree
> Undecided
>   protest
>   This planet"

By coming toward you with the horn behind;†
Those sieves he made of poetry's 'Golden Bowls'
By knocking comprehension full of holes;
These all he piled upon the Hindu pyre,
Then topped them with a most ambitious spire,
His last divestment and his final measure,
The blueprint that had augured so much pleasure:
To build a Moog Machine that fills the air
With *Correspondances* of Baudelaire
By hitching up the sundry human senses
To some computer that in turn condenses
All Cosmos to a lone compounded word
That through the use of sensors could be heard!††
    Then this, his eulogy: "O, Dullness, I
Must blow your cover just to say 'Goodbye!'
The others could not find you though they seek,

---

†'unicorns conceived to bend the mind':
"There is no day in the calendar
The dairy company sent out
That lets you possess it wildly like
The body of a dreaming woman in a dream:
All flop over at the top when seized,
The stem too slender, the top too loose and heavy, . . ."
                    —from "Hop O' My Thumb," p. 32.

††With the blueprint for his Moog Machine, John again demonstrated an uncanny prescience worthy of Tom Swift himself. Just recently, which would make it more than ten years after John's stay in France, I saw a machine very much like this actually unveiled on television. I have none of John's mechanical aptitude for such things, but it seemed to work like this: Mathematical values were given to certain words with their equivalents in sound and color. The values were synthesized in a scientific equation. This was extrapolated into a computer attached to a Moog-like Machine. Finally, the print-out could be picked up as either poem, picture or music, which bore some presumed relationship to Baudelaire's *Correspondances*. John Cage undoubtedly knows all about such electronic experiments with art. More than likely he has discussed them with John Ashbery and many other people by this time. But back in the sixties, it would seem that John had been truly prophetic.

Behind your change of lifestyles every week;
But I, in secret, served your cause so well
I'd rather bid myself than you 'Farewell!'
Ambition found the ice of patience thin,
This falling-out, preferred to falling-in!
Since Einstein conquered by the sun's eclipse,†
I thought I'd blot out mind with my ellipse;††
And since the pits and runnels of the worst
Become an eminence, I'd get there first
To reinforce the jolts of Future Shock
By stepping-up the volts of fancy schlock;
With all the Segals, Bachs and all the Dalis
Just charge Admission to our Empire Follies;†††

---

†A proof of Einstein's Relativity was provided by the famous eclipse (in India during the late 30s?) that demonstrated light rays did indeed bend when passing by a large mass.

††Ashbery's most prevalent poetic device is an extended ellipse, an intriguing kind of obscurantism that rights itself at the last precarious minute. This is kept as loose as possible to allow entry of the 'confusion and chaos of modern life.' In describing his own work for an encyclopedia of 'Contemporary Poets,' Ashbery has written: "The outlook is Romantic . . . Characteristic devices are ellipses, frequent changes of tone, voice (that is, the narrator's voice), point of view, to give an impression of flux."

In the name of these ellipses, Ashbery opens himself to the charge of willful obscurity, which he invariably answers by a kind of default: "The difficulty of my poetry . . . is meant to reflect the difficulty of living." Here, I believe, his sophistry borders on a more onerous hypocrisy. I believe he is fully aware that he skirts close to the fatal quicksand of the Pathetic Fallacy and yet will not concede his readers the integrity of their own logic. This may turn out to be an immoral imposition on the thousands of young students who are now writing Ashbery-like verse on campuses all across the country. Surely, if Nature, according to the Pathetic Fallacy, does not share our human feelings, it cannot share our 'confusion' and 'difficulty with being alive.' Ashbery criticism—God help us!—will finally settle on this one great weakness in his work.

†††Like Erich Segal, Richard Bach and the painter S. Dali, Ashbery tries to reach that wide elitist audience that affects literacy and refinement without realizing what is actually involved. I mean, the ones who feel that Erich Segal's *Love Story* and Bach's *Seagull* and Dali's paintings are 'art' in the great tradition.

And give the scholiasts some stuff to chew on,
As Nero gnawed Decline to utter Ruin!†
Dereglement de tous les sens humains††
Provides no *moola pour le vin* or *pain*;
Perverse 'farewell' is eased by *lack* of 'grease':
I got more pay for just a press release;†††
So much for nothing, Dullness, this must do;
In several languages, I bid 'Adieu!'
Rimbaud and I must go exclusive ways,
He drunken, I but in my usual daze!
   "I hereby from this stubborn, exiled ground
Warn Simon that I won't be 'kicked around!'††††
That he must find another boy to thrash,
Lest anal critics lack for petty cash;
Or better yet, take up croquet instead

---

†". . . Zealous research scholars, scouting for abstruse areas of investigation, have already descended on him (Ashbery) for the mere joy of Confrontation with 'obscurity in its densest form.' " English-Indian critic Shiv Kumar in *Span*, a U.S. Government publication printed in India.

††Much of John's formal study has been in French. So he knows Rimbaud's admonition to poets: To systematically induce their own madness. Having tried it, at this point he doesn't care whether he quotes the Frenchman exactly.

†††In the early '50s, Ashbery worked 9 to 5 for the Oxford University Press in New York, writing press releases.

††††The all-pervasive, all-purpose elite critic for all time, John Simon, wrote in the *Hudson Review* of Ashbery's *The Tennis Court Oath* (1962): "Mr Ashbery has perfected his verse to the point where it never deviates into—nothing so square as sense!—sensibility, sensuality, or sentences." As an undoubted member of the more-or-less self-appointed National Book Critics Circle, which gave Ashbery's *Self-Portrait* top honors in 1976 (despite the fact that some members of this body I have talked with deny ever having read, not only his poetry but any poetry since their college days), Simon probably realizes that he and Ashbery have more than first names in common: as purveyors of boredom on a national scale for important dollars in the prints, at colleges and on the lecture circuit.

Or have another meal upon his head!†
I'll send my misbegotten bardic soul
Straight up this Paris chimney's flaming hole
And pray the fumes afflict such misanthropes
Until they *really* choke upon my tropes!
You found my verse much too obscure to please?
They said the same of Legionnaire's Disease!††
En garde, mes freres! I bend now to the task
As Parma took a cane to every flask!"†††
Then with a canny smile and quirky kick,
He leaned right over and he 'flicked his Bic';
Then up in flames it went, his total 'oeuvre':
This 'Painter's' work at last would reach the Louvre!
   The fire crept over all: His childhood rhyme
Curled up in drowsy smoke, still counting time;††††
His "Europe,"††††† limp from lack of verbal tissue,

---

†'another meal upon his head': In the mid-70s, an actress who felt especially victimized by Simon's chronic venom dumped a plate of food on his head during a theatre or movie party at, was it Sardi's?

††'Legionnaire's Disease': One theory holds this disease that claimed scores of lives at a Philadelphia Legion Convention in 1976 was conveyed in the form of smoke through the heat ducts of the hotel. John bitterly dreams that the smoke from his mss. may have a similar impact on his critics.

†††Parma here is short for Parmigiano. It is not difficult to imagine the embittered painter smashing the flasks, beakers and retorts in his lab after alchemy betrayed him into debt, oblivion and the prospect of an 'ignominious death.'

††††'His childhood rhyme, etc.': We learn that Ashbery assisted his friend David K. Kermani (to whom *Self-Portrait* is dedicated) compile *John Ashbery: A Comprehensive Bibliography* (1975), which has enough unpublished poetry for at least 20 volumes. "It's not going to be published, if I have anything to say about it," the poet told Kostelanetz. May we exercise so much prudence as to imagine that the matter eventually might elude his proscription. The oblivion of his juvenilia, however, he insists, has been happily achieved: "I burned all my high-school poetry a few years ago," John assures us.

†††††"Europe" (1960), a *tour de force* of acoherence, splintered syntax and associational mayhem, has already been described.

Could not avoid at least *one* burning issue;
The *magma* from his 'Rivers' and his 'Mountains'†
Erupted now in piffling, hissing fountains;
His *Tennis Court*,†† which at the net had snorted,
Now found the set so heatedly aborted;
The Double Dream of Spring,††† whose mirrored stare
Saw triple Aprils from the barber's chair,
Which for its title should have been destroyed,
Beyond the Eiffel Tower was now deployed;
Three Poems,†††† assembled from the limbs of prose,
Toward saner incarnations now arose;
Each sparkling tidbit up the chimney shinnies,
The myriad playlets with *A Nest of Ninnies!*†††††
O, never were such masterpieces scorched

---

†*Rivers and Mountains* (1966) brought John away from the disjunctions of much of his earlier work and marks a turning-point in critical acceptance.

"Why it should all boil down to one
Uniform substance, a magma of interiors."
—from "Self-Portrait," p. 71.

††*The Tennis Court Oath* (1962).
†††*The Double Dream of Spring* (1971).
††††"The next transformation of his creative career," Kostelanetz tells us, "was a book modestly entitled *Three Poems*(1972), which took the radical provocative step of being written entirely in prose." Ashbery takes up the narrative: "I used prose because I'm constantly trying to think of things I haven't done yet, and prose poetry until that point, as in Baudelaire or Rimbaud, always seemed slightly askew and not quite right. It sort of sounds self-conscious and 'poetic,' a quality I dislike in prose. I was wondering: What about writing prose poetry in which the ugliness of prose would be exploited and put to the uses of poetry? And that was hard to do, of course, like everything." Ashbery 'explains' further: "There is a great deal of prose in *Three Poems* that is pompous, awkward, self-consciously poetic, like the prose poetry I was trying to get away from. I wanted to use these things which were unpoetic materials in something I could consider a poem, and I feel I succeeded there." Judging by my copy of the poems, the entire matter remains in doubt. *Three Poems*, however, is Ashbery's favorite book, predictably, you might say.
†††††Though now writing a 'long play,' John says he wants none of his many

Since Caesar had both Greece and Egypt torched!
   Which to undo, great Dullness was aroused,
To save the Laureate she had just espoused:
She hopped upon her trusty mattress warmer,
Whose shape and size inspired the Backfire Bomber,
And as the winds our longitudes elide,
She heaved herself to Paris and his side!
Her presence in his room soon stifled all,
John's siege of sense and the ensuing pall:
She wiggled once and wooed him with his name;
The mirror was restored; so sank the flame!
The poet wakened as the mortal slept;
Then down the Paris skies the Goddess swept
By laser beam with only brief ado
From Paris to New York, where John came to
Within her bunker and her mighty arms,
To cheers and tributes *and* police alarms!
The Goddess had, you see, to Koch confided,
A son of Cibber would be soon provided:
Then Koch told Kornblee, Kornblee, Cott,
Cott, Kostelanetz, who just told the lot!†
The wily Goddess knew no public line
Spread secrets faster than her college vine.

---

early playlets to be produced. He has also collaborated with poet James Schuyler in writing a 'charming' (Kostelanetz's word) novel, *A Nest of Ninnies* (1969).

---

†Of his return to New York (1966), Kostelanetz writes: "An unknown poet a decade before, he returned a conquering hero, sort of. During his absence, he was still a presence in New York. The art dealer Jill Kornblee remembers, 'Everybody talked about him as though he were in the room.' His reading at the Living Theatre drew a packed house. Kenneth Koch, by then a professor of English at Columbia College, had introduced Ashbery's work to his students; one of them, Jonathan Cott, wrote the first extended critical consideration of Ashbery's poetry for an anthology of criticism which I edited, *The New American Arts* (1965), in which Cott identified Ashbery as 'today's most radically original American poet.' " What a small world!

And so upon that fabled day of days
Ashbery, John sat up to sudden praise,
And found his suite could boast of more display
Than all the auction rooms at Parke-Bernet!†
Motif of crême, cerise and citrus shade:
"O, this will match my poem on lemonade!"††
He cried, obliquely lest we all forget,
He turns 'hello'††† into a whole 'Quartet'!
Quoth he: "I'll say a piece I just call "Fame":
"Yours is a house that bears another's name,
Where neighbors come and seem to pay the rent
And leave me change from dough I never spent;
It's not the place I did not want to be,
And not the place I rather hoped to see,

---

†The Goddess was simply making Ashbery finally feel he had found a home. Kostelanetz describes Ashbery's apartment on New York's Lower West Side: "Clearly the residence of a cultivated man, it has antique furniture, fine rugs, Chinese porcelain, exquisite Persian rugs, lamps, plants, flowers, shelves of books, hundreds of records and a glass table filled with literary magazines, in addition to prints and paintings by his friends, etc . . ."

Again, for a man whose poetry utterly disparages material things and all the practical accomplishments of the past and present and all hope for the future, this collection of material ballast presents some sort of amazing irony.

†† "Come once and for all into our
   Consideration though it be flat like *lemonade*." (Italics added)
                                      —from "Robin Hood's Barn", p. 62.

†††Saying 'hello' can be a big deal to this poet:

   "There is no way of knowing whether these are
   Our neighbors or friendly savages trapped in the distance
   By the red tape of a mirage. The fact that
   We drawled 'hallo' to them just lazily enough this morning
   Doesn't mean that a style was inaugurated. Anyway evening
   Kind of changes things. Not the color,
   The quality of a handshake, the edge of someone's breath
   So much as a general anxiety to get everything all added up,
   Flowers arranged and out of sight."
                                      —from "No Way of Knowing," p. 56.

But where I've never been and somehow miss,
Where now I'm going though it's not like this:
In short, the place I spoke of by extension
So vaguely that I did not really mention,
Which makes it in-between, not bad, not good:
How's *this* for poetry *and* how *is* the food?"†
   His friends all cheered and railed and shared a smile
To find him fat on poems of self-denial:
Then he: "These accidents without contusions,††
My poems, drop words and lines and all conclusions:
Disparity suggests a modern schism;†††
A shattered mind, a new Exoticism!
Not Swift, Defoe and not Voltaire perhaps,††††

---

†That Ashbery really talks like this, we learn from the Kostelanetz interview, where the poet further explains his "Europe": " 'I didn't want to write the poetry that was coming naturally to me then,' he explained, typically speaking in negatives, 'and I succeeded in writing something that wasn't the poetry I didn't want to write, and yet was not the poetry I wanted to write.' "

††'Accidents without contusions' seems a more accurate description of Existential poetry than M. Moore's 'real toads in imaginary gardens.'

†††The split in modern sensibility perceived by Eliot has been hyperbolized to a Grand Canyon in Ashbery. While it is true that the Cartesian and Newtonian descriptions of linear interactions and direct causal relationships may be no longer adequate, it is equally true that purposive gibberish is not an analogue for modern relativism.

††††Where Swift, Defoe and Voltaire (and many others) invoked exotic places where the new notions of man's perfectibility might be demonstrated, Ashbery tries to suggest that a creative individuality might be achieved through bizarre perceptions and an esthetic grounded entirely in the human mind's capacity to always imagine it is somewhere else. On this, Ashbery quotes one Sydney Freedberg on Parmigiano:

". . . Realism in this portrait
No longer produces an objective truth, but a *bizarria* . . ."
                                           —from "Self-Portrait," p. 73.

Or, later in the same poem he invokes human companionship in a world of clothes and furniture, and says:

"This could have been our paradise: exotic
Refuge within an exhausted world, . . ." (p. 82)

But then again, there's been a ripping lapse:
Not only taste this time, but sense is past;
Banality is basic, bound to last!"†
They clapped and cheered some more and chaired him forth
Above the 'freebies' and the punch's froth!
Our lettered stars had come from everywhere,
Much to their booking-agents foul despair:††
Bob Bly, in macho, rubber poncho stood,
Still redolent of Minnesota's wood;†††
Kinnell, who'd evidently checked his bear,
Flashed reputation like a shock of hair;††††
And Howard Moss, who had an awful jag on,
Wept openly to learn he'd lost his wagon;†††††
Joyce Carol Oates began a book-length ballad

---

†Ashbery exudes an impudent and airy manner that characterizes many of
our more intelligent artists today, though once it was openly scorned as the
cynicism of the dilettante.
††Poetry readings and residencies at colleges constitute a multi-million dollar
business in the U.S., involving relatively a few poets, all of whom know each
other and conspire quite openly to further their mutual ends through cross-
recommendations in the overlapping spheres of teaching, publishing and
poetry reading. It is virtually impossible to break into this world without the
collusion of those already there. The favoritism here is much more morbid and
incestuous than in either show business or politics. Poetry, however, is held in
such low esteem by the general public that the movies and other media have
not bothered to satirize the situation.
†††It is understood that Robert Bly lives in some sort of frontier structure in a
wooded area of his home state of Minnesota. It figures.
††††Galway Kinnell, the Swan of the Seekonk River (near Pawtucket, R.I.,
where he was reared in deep reverence for Yeats), has made a great impression
on the college reading circuit with his rendering of his "The Bear" epic, where
he plays all parts to the hilt, or, we might say, to the forelock.
†††††As an occasional visitor to Fire Island, Howard Moss is well-acquainted
with the little red grocery wagons tenants use there. We imagine here that he
grew so fond of his own that he took it with him wherever he went, even into
Manhattan.

While passing sullen Rich the Caesar's salad;†
And Merwin, who would now the Orient know,
Had two imported Geisha girls in tow;††
While Malcolm Brinnin, rescued from the stacks,†††
Found fame had fled with all the Cheese-It! snacks!
    Then Dullness called from where in state she sat:
"All hail to great King John, our Laureate!"
As Plebes for luck award Tecumseh's head,
They cheered and waved and threw him catered bread!††††
"Hail John!" arose with Perrier and Schweppes,
And echoed from afar on Monty's steps!†††††
"All hail!" resounded from great Kaufman Hall, ††††††
"Long may he wave!" sang bells from Berkeley's mall!
"Stop presses!" ventured Poetry magazine;
"We'll book him early!" beamed each college green:†††††††

---

†Surely Joyce Carol must compose while doing things like passing salads.
She threatens all records in published garrulity. Adrienne Rich has placed her
entire sense of humor, and many other pleasant emotions, in escrow for the
duration of the Women's Liberation Movement, which may outlast both her
sanity and the public's patience.
††W.S. Merwin apparently makes it his practice to patronize women
brought up in the cultures he happens to be studying. Right now (August,
1977), it's the Orient, including Hawaii.
†††Since his heyday as Dylan Thomas's Horatio, Brinnin has spent more and
more time in obscurity among the 'stacks,' either the smokestacks of old ocean
liners or the bookstacks of old libraries.
††††Annapolis midshipmen toss money at the statue of Tecumseh for luck.
†††††Monty's steps are the steps of the Lamont Library at Harvard.
††††††Kaufman Hall is the Y.H.M.A., East Coast poetry headquarters.
†††††††The award of a Pulitzer triggers off a mass reaction at colleges across the
country to book the 'celebrated poet' for lectures and readings.

All prayed he'd be the Existential Rage
And Optical Illusion of the Age!
So, Hail, O Thane of Torpor,† Hail! And look!
How Butler's Alma Mater drops her book!††

---

†In Macbeth the Witches divulge part of their prophecy by hailing the hero as
'Thane of Cawdor!' The slight alteration above becomes part of *this* prophecy.
††John got his M.A. at Columbia University. In front of the Butler Library
there, the great statue entitled 'Alma Mater' sits with a huge book opened wide
in her robed lap. The news of John's coronation so shocks her that she drops
this symbol of learning.

BOOK THE FOURTH

Argument

The King being proclaimed, the Solemnity is graced with Public Games and Sports of Various Kinds. The Book World is represented by All its Functionaries: the Savants, the Booksellers, the Patrons, and, of course, the Poets in Force. King John is glorious in the Midst of this, dispensing Honors and winning Prizes, as Kings usually do. The Goddess first conducts the Games for Publishers' Representatives; then those for the Patrons and Writers. Next, Competition between Poets. Finally, the Critics' Conclave, which ends the Day, whereat All depart, weary and fulfilled.

Great Homer and his pupil Virgil told
How once the King was vested with his gold,
Ensuing dawn should find the populace
Restored to honor and a state of grace,
Which to attest, the gods should then decree
A day of games and sports and public spree,
To bring the Monarch's diverse subjects 'round
To firm their purpose on some common ground,
And let their King behold them all as one,
As different flowers alike must share the sun.
Achilles and Aeneas both had done this once,
And so, Pope tells us, had the other Dunce:†
'Twas thus we find King John enthroned in state
In Central Park upon an orange crate!
The Goddess had proposed 'your standard throne,'
But then as now, John's choice was all his own.
The Meadow†† that had suffered such distress
At gross New Yorkers and their 'perfect mess,'
Had quaked with every trauma, every shock,
From protest marches to unruly Rock,
Awoke from sharing death with Olmsted's dream†††
To face the living hell called 'Academe!'
    Not even 'winos' trespass at that hour.
Before the sun bathes Gulf & Western's tower,
And yet, from God knows where! they had arrived,

---

†Colley Cibber. See *The Dunciad*, the opening of Book II.
††The Sheep Meadow in Central Park.
†††Frederick Law Olmsted, America's greatest landscape architect, whose masterpiece of "Democratic Design" was Central Park, which has all but been destroyed by the presumptuous patrons and politicians, who never bothered to grasp Olmsted's inspired 'poetic' concept of the park as a work of master craftmanship and great art. They have donated so many 'polluting' artifacts and facilities that soon there will be little more than a small open plot of unsullied grassland with a plaque announcing 'Here once stood Central Park.' Sic transit gloria!

As bees from great removes have often hived:
Ten-thousand strong they came, by ones and scores,
The Book World's mighty, awful, myriad bores!
Anthologers ad-hoc! Bold poetasters!
Propounders most pro-tem! Proud paper-wasters!
Savants in residence, bald men on grants,
The males in breezy shorts, the women pants!
By moped, limo', bike and bouncing van,
They took that 'Leyte' as by battle-plan!
    A sorry lot of every sort they were,
The kind who wear those badges at the fair,
In case they should get lost from all the rest,
Can find out who they are right off their chest:
Instructors, each with desperate Ph D,
Embuttressed John and throne on bended knee,
While *full* professors clutched their salutations,
Like choc'late soldiers at inaug'ral stations!
Though vast the field, their ranks were tight, alas!
'The College Wedge,' it's called, for kissing ass!
As odd King John, that Laureate! That Dunce!
Wrung pounds of pomp from palms that weigh an ounce:
For him, a finger, her, an eyebrow raised,
For each, that Protean face, as Cibber gazed,
First grim, enslaved by thought, then bold and affable,
But always myst'ry-riddled, always laughable!

He left them all to guess just what he thinks,
As hometown hopes address the desert sphinx!
   The multi-national 'reps' in force were there,
Those tax-free patrons of Endowment's chair,
The final arbiters of Book Awards,
Whose bucks 'cut mustard' just like swords;
Those 'judges' of our Science, Arts and Letters,
In lieu of 'overlooking' all their betters,
Just lolled with Mark and Archie† on the grass,
And watched a galaxy of Frisbees pass!
The Harvard crew linked arms for Ivy nexus,††
To check the flow of power toward oil-rich Texas,
While scribes from Baylor U and Austin Falls
Showed up in silver-buttoned overalls,
And schools from Florida, self-dubbed 'The East,'
Seemed overjoyed to find the Park at least!
   O, what a day that now would soon begin!
As morning waxed and then affixed its grin:
On Plimpton,††† free-lance clown from *chez* Elaine
And Dry Dock Country, with his jingling train;
Broyard, ††††apostate grand, and Peck's Bad Boy,
With pen and pad equipped, to kill some joy;

---

†Mark Van Doren and Archibald MacLeish.
††The majority of our most visible poets either studied or taught at Harvard
University. There is abundant evidence that virtually all of them had a hand in
helping the careers of the others through the lucrative world of American let-
ters. That's probably the main reason we've heard so much about them. That's
the way it works. Now they seem most anxious, lest literary leverage move to
the Southwest due to the strong attraction of higher teaching salaries and
grants. Among the nervous Harvard bunch, a few that come to mind: John
Ashbery, John Brinnin, Robert Bly, John Ciardi, Tom Combs, Richard
Eberhart, Robert Fitzgerald, Donald Hall, John Hollander, Kenneth Koch,
Stanley Kunitz, Archibald MacLeish, Howard Nemerov, George Starbuck,
Richard Wilbur, and many others.
†††George Plimpton, gentleman dilettante and kibitzer.
††††Anatole Broyard, who quit writing his own stuff with a vengeance, and

Grace Schulman, sudden, city-wide sensation,
By virtue of some holdings in *The Nation*,†
In black to show her pearls from toe to hood,
Close by the all-embracing Goddess stood,
As Howard,†† with his Hunter 'groupies' near,
Said something clever for the crowd to hear;
And Lita Hornick, with her entourage,
Upon a squeaking float of Cleo's barge,
With G. Malanga and Giorno came,†††
As if arriving for the Rose Bowl Game,
While Harold Bloom from Yale, with eighty tyros,
Descended in a gale of Coast Guard gyros!
   Alerted to the 'weirdos' on the green,
The Marshal posted signs of 'quarantine,'
Not soon enough to check the 'Parrot Flu'
That felled a hippo' at the nearby zoo!
No matter then, the gods were so behooved
The Goddess now like Bella Abzug moved,
Against whose progress all the gathering gave,
As Tokyo tankers shrug aside the wave,
And gained a hillock, fired an antique gun,
As King John stood, the games had thus begun:
So by the text, she gave the race a whirl,

---

then heaped his bitterness on those who saw no reason to quit, through his book reviews in the N.Y. *Times*. Now (1977) that he's writing again himself, his critical tone has softened noticeably.

---

†Her greatest critical contribution to date has been the declaration that the Viet Nam War cancelled the logic of using metaphor in verse. Vosnesensky remains much closer to a poetic reality when he hails metaphor as 'the engine of the poem.'
††Poet Richard Howard.
†††Lita Hornick, critic and patron of the arts, former editor of *Kulchur Magazine*, now publisher of *Kulchur Books*, has called King John, in effect, our greatest poet, excepting possibly John Giorno, whose *Cancer in My Left Ball*

Where Juno tricked out Turnus, Pope, his Curl,†
By turning out a phantom of a poet
So publishers with 'guts' would 'race' to show it.
And yet with actual poets make-believe,
Who needs a conjured bard so to deceive:
Their lives are more unreal in every bit
Than any phantom Pope or Virgil hit.
   So Merwin from the crowd was summoned forth,
Whose shape and air suggest the phantóm's froth:
The dimpled cheek, the dappled wreath of hair,
So boned you wonder whether brain is there,
The cloven hoof, the coat of velveteen,
The pretty, pastel poems with swampfire's sheen!
"Anality, the bullhorn, dear!" the Goddess called:
"Who with my Muses, who with 'Buddha's balled,'††
Who'll raise the flag of Schuster or of Day,
To outrun all and take this prize away?"
"T'is I, O Goddess, of the House of Random,
Who'll catch that prize on skateboard or on tandem!"
Had he his way, the 'Rep' would not have spoken,
Whose voice at work remained, at most, a token;
Who as a mail clerk had been loudly fired,
And then, 'to head up poetry,' was rehired;
Who kept his inter-office memos terse
When forced to justify his choice of verse,

---

and *Balling Buddha* she published. Gerard Malanga, bard of the Jet Set, oracle for The Beautiful People, is also in her stable. Giorno is known, if at all, as an exponent of 'found poetry,' a la 'found sculpture.'

---

†Both Virgil and Pope use apparitions to distract their villains: as Juno, Turnus in *The Aeneid*, so the Goddess sets before Curl, the greedy bookseller, a phantom poet, which he vainly chases to end with nothing.
††As noted, *Balling Buddha* is the title of one of John Giorno's books of verse, published by *Kulchur Books*.

Because he'd read no book at all since school,
And left decisions to the typing pool;
If asked, was prone to think an 'ancient lay'
Was tossed-off by Macaulay 'in the hay!'
And as for Merwin, he would just evade him,
Except that RCA so well had paid him
To make the public think the Sarnoff vulture
Still had a talon left for US culture!

   "Who'll meet the challenge of my bold pursuit
Of What's-His-Name decked-out in poet's boot?"
He called again. "Just bite your foaming bit,"
The Goddess joshed, "and read the PR kit
My Muses have prepared with tears and treacle:
This race is won on foot and not on vehicle!"
In fear the others froze with nervous cough;
Then came the challenge, "I!" It was Knopf!
A houndless hunt they'd hold, with only foxes,
Since RCA owned both, like Chinese boxes;
While one must win, the other could not lose,
As in their samplings of press conf'rence booze.

   But with the contest set, fleet Merwin sped,
As first Knopf, then Random forged ahead:
Now for a moment they were nip-and-tuck,
As Merwin lept aboard a pick-up truck;
The Goddess shouted, "Foul!" admonished all,

To "Come out fighting now, come on, play ball!"
At which the poet then forthwith desisted,
To prove he could be fair and still two-fisted:
Now down the cindered bridal path he ripped,
As Random cut some corners, Knopf then tripped!
"Who follows me," Bill crowed, "I've got to spoil it!"
By way of detour through a public toilet!
Then out again and over piles of litter,
He broke for daylight with a shout and skitter!
Then scaled a bench, and dashed across the Mall,
Which stunned King John, and left the crowd in thrall!
   O, Merwin now, a thing of many splendors!
Wove in and out through all those startled vendors,
So far ahead he stopped right in his course
To feed some leaves to one patrolman's horse,
And snapped off flowers along his dazzling way,
And taunted all with "I'm Queen of the May!"
The which to prove, he scampered up a boulder,
And struck a cheesecake pose with brazen shoulder!
Last seen, entranced by Merwin's metric maze,
The 'Reps,' reduced to listless, feckless daze,
Loped off dejected, as if bound for hell,
As Merwin vanished by the Music Shell!
   The 'Reps' kept right on going, per their praxis,
Back to the office, via separate taxis:

Knopf had several salesmen's hands to crunch
Before retiring to his three-hour lunch,
While Random with the phones played hide-and-seek,
Banged out two memos, and took off a week!
Now Merwin by this time was lost indeed,
So strange had been his course, so great his speed!
Since much like Hansel, he could not get back,
He let his *sutras* just suggest a track:
He first as flutist from those Grecian urns
Piped 'Bonnie Doon' before the bronze of Burns,†
Then took heroic Balto for a walk,
En route besieging Scott with deadly talk;
He now mistook a rock for Merton's Mountain,††
And forged the Helispont in' Thesda's Fountain;†††
Then once aboard an empty battered boat,
Across the Rowing Lake began to float;
By 'Venice Bridges,' he just 'ups and dies,'
Much to a group of muggers' stark surprise!
Then as a clump of earth hove into sight,
He claimed for Kaufman Hall the Isle of Wight!
By 'passage trial,' as Hercules before,
Or Old MacArthur, he just strode ashore!
Where two balloon men with their tanks of air
Like double Buddhas so engaged his stare
He had to buy a bunch of red†††† balloons,

---

†Merwin covers a lot of ground. On the Mall in Central Park, there are bronze statues of Robert Burns and Sir Walter Scott. Not far away, there is a life-sized bronze of Balto, the dog who delivered a crucial serum to Nome, Alaska.
††Thomas Merton wrote the highly-esteemed religious tract, *Seven Storey Mountain.* Some of Merwin's verse has overtones of an anemic mysticism.
†††Bethesda's Fountain is located near the Central Park Rowing Lake.
††††Red is the favorite color of the Existential poets. They also like 'calico clouds,' uncut pages of a book and any kind of reflection, as noted earlier.

And name them all his 'Pets' or 'Chinese moons';
Then climbed aboard a 'horse' and gave a yell
Of "Hi-ho, Tantra!" from the carousel!
　Meanwhile, the Goddess, John, the fete, in fine,
So vainly dwelt upon that finish line!
Yet since their epics made such frequent use
Of voided meaning and abortive ruse,
They viewed the ending in the course of time
As fitting both their Age and lack of rhyme.
As Nash might say: "The race need not have finish,
Or middle, just because it has beginnish!"
Besides, this Age can't sense how bookmen sprinted
In times of Pope to get their poets printed!
The stuff of verse was Ford's communal 'glue';†
For one, A. Pope accrued one million due.††
The form today's so stamped with 'precious' school,
It wins 'malign neglect'††† or ridicule!
These painter-poets write such vapid verse,
The House that prints it risks eternal curse!
Like Flags, they run-up poets through the year,
And yet would pay them more to disappear!
The public, tuned to call the umpires 'liars,'
Descries a 'Foul!" in phony versifiers,
And won't give up its baseball, beer or mutton
For ballads on the Buddha's belly-button,

†President Ford once referred to something, probably his own Presidency, as being the 'social glue' that held things together. In Pope's day, poetry went a long way to serve this purpose, though today poetry, through its specialization by the Existentialists and academics, has become an absolute irrelevancy.
††Pope made what would now amount to almost one-million dollars from his various epics in his lifetime, his translations of Homer, etc.
†††This, of course, is a variation on Senator Patrick Moynihan's suggestion that the indigent blacks in this country should be regarded with 'benign neglect,' one of the most venal episodes in the Nixon Administration's pronouncement-making, which has not received its due attention, mainly

Though campuses, like girls in heat, are wallowing
To hand the Merry Men of John their following!
   In truth, the Goddess had been gratified
To lend a semblance that its sales belied:
That poetry in the market-place is viable,
Not some *pariah* for which all are liable,
So dull it can not even cause a scandal,
Much less a race that might be worth the candle!
   Yet still we give the day and Devil due:
The Goddess, John, the crowd, as if on cue,
Turned southward toward an urgent roar,
As through the fields, exploding dust before,
With all the dash and verve of Sherman's horses,
Fell swift the squadrons of her mobile forces!
"My rolling-stock!" she cried. "My Bookmobiles!
That wed the love of words to love of wheels!
Behold!" "Run for your life!" she should have said,
For once they'd past, they counted twenty dead!
Len Randolph and his aides in surplus Jeeps
Enjoined them onward with their waves and beeps;
Right through the frenzied crowd they blazed and thundered,
Recalling films of Indy's famed Five-hundred!
They'd speed prodigious miles before the dark,
Still looking for a legal place to park!
They're now a 'must,' these 'shops' with brake and clutch,

---

because the American people in their misanthropy largely accepted
Moynihan's sadistic attitude; a presentiment of this popular approval might be
what allowed him to express the notion in the first place.

For any Fund that's worth the name as such,
Though roadside sales at fairs in fields and thickets
Can't quite offset the cost of traffic tickets!
    The Muses scurried forth about the field,
Assessing losses that their count might yield:
The dead: two poets of West Coast cachet,
In bits and pieces like their syntax lay;
Two Yale 'men' writing 'tomes' on Critic Bloom,
Among so many, Yale could use the room;
Old 'Doc,' who haunted halls at Iowa State,
Now learned that 'never' *was* much worse than 'late';
One 'Prof' from Tufts, whose 'friends,' despite display,
Had almost clapped to find him 'on his way';
Two parasites from Brown, or something worse,
Made good their pledge: 'To give their all to verse';
An ancient salesman from Farrar-Giroux,
With final words: "God, what a way to go!"
Among the wounded, there were some in shock,
So like themselves as to escape remark!
And as the roll was called, with sobs and wrenches,
Bloom ran about expounding 'War and Trenches'!†
    With cries of 'Medic!' thus the Muses went,
Removing bodies to the rubbish tent,
Until the Goddess, irked by such delay,
Demanded that the games get underway:

---

†Harold Bloom has tried to make a separate art, a special branch of learning, not so much of criticism in general, but of his own criticism in particular, by formulating arcane nomenclature and exotic categories of appraisal projected by him personally from his blind at Yale. Consequently, just as Ashbery has all of collegiate America writing poems like his, Yale undergraduates now face the task of criticising his, Bloom's, criticism of people like, now guess, John Ashbery! That's right! Bloom thinks he's 'apt to last.' One of Bloom's theories concerns his willful misreading of poets, which he has described as a kind of 'defensive warfare.' He labors greatly to stress the agonies of this warfare and has likened the critics' work today to the perils of hand-to-hand combat, by implication, in 'the trenches.'

Her all-important authors' trials were set,
Whereby the poets vie to see what cash they'll get:
As source of funds, the Landed and the Lord
Had been replaced by School and Corporate Board,
And so instead of trial by 'tickling feather,'†
She simply used the social get-together,
Where poetry's streams today break-in their beds,
And future currents find their Nile-like heads!
To which effect, the Goddess brought much sand,
To simulate the drift of beach or strand,
Of off-shore isle, or key, or everglade,
Where next year's reputations will be made;
A dune at Pines,†† the Cape, or Catalina,
Where Pulitzers assume their bright patina;
Where arbiters decide what *was* and *wasn't*,
And *who* knows *whom* and who just *doesn't*,
Cut patterns as to what to print or teach,
Like New York garmentmen at Ocean Beach!†††
    She'd set the seascape scene so rather well,
With crunched-up beer can and with cast-off shell,
Umbrellas, blankets and the radio's blare,
A few stripped quite beyond their underwear,
And went in search of surf, or took a stroll
Like Vic McLaglen in "The Lost Patrol!"

---

†Pope's poets in *The Dunciad* compete by tickling the palm of the patron with their quills. The poets today engage in a more highly socialized kind of tickling, as described above.
††The Pines is a colony on Fire Island, N.Y. By Cape, of course, I mean to include Provincetown, Hyannis, Martha's Vineyard, Nantucket, where much of this sort of thing goes on.
†††Ocean Beach, by far the largest settlement on Fire Island, is known as the watering-spot for thousands of workers from Manhattan's garment district every summer.

But most of course would use this fond event
To seal their sinecures with fresh cement:
The blanket-hopping on that single day
Sent hundreds on their destined, bardic way,
And showed by many duneside coup and sandswept round
How poets' names advance on shifty ground:
For instance, take that youth from LIU,
Who turned a pretty frank at barbecue;
He brushed against some shirtless Big Eight† scribes,
And on the basis of such beachside 'vibes,'
Was later published in the Big Review
As *the* exponent of New York haiku;
His school would duly note the able 'hit,'
And name him head of English-Chinese Lit!
   How cutely met the 'rube' and New York 'wheel,'
Whose chance encounter meant a three-way deal:
Warm smiles exuded, lotions were exchanged,
Exposing interests, meetings then arranged,
When in the fall the poet would secure
A grant or two, perhaps a reading tour,
And guarantee the 'wheel' as recompense,
His school's rich offer of a 'residence,'
And through the efforts of a mutual friend,
They'd launch a nation-wide poetic trend!
How well the Goddess used that panorama

---

†The once highly-touted Big Eight reviews include: *Partisan, Massachusetts, Sewanee, Shenendoah, Hudson, Kenyon* (defunct), *Chicago, Prairie Schooner.*

To bare the innards of the noxious drama,
While Muses, garbed as Romans, did their stint,
Dispensing vodkas with a sprig of mint!
The hottest beds of interest, now as then,
Find Moss and Ginsberg bucking up their men,
And cudgeling both Institute and Fund
To give their proteges the cummerbund,
To Corso, say, as some belated 'beat,'
Or Merrill for his cold aesthetic feat,
While Hornick and the zombies she espouses
With private cash bring plague on both their houses!
   Perhaps the Goddess had been ill-advised
To make her replica so well-devised:
The sex and liquor, like a bomb-burst 'round,
Drove all her legions to the blasted ground,
Where now with clasp of hand and purse of lips
They sealed the pacts that void rejection slips,
To publish, teach or read, show-up to hear,
Forecasting fashions for the coming year!
Most sluggish now they were to meet her call
Of "Onward, to the Ramble! Onward, all!"
And yet they followed with their wills of iron,
That Piper with her prizes, bells and siren:
Her forces flooded forth, those thousands strong,
Tugged muggers, kids and oldsters, tramps along,

And reached the Ramble on the Park's West Side,
Which, know, had once been Olmsted's deepest pride,
A place of perfect peace, a citadel,
A paradise within Manhattan's hell!
Its ruin now, its nudity, attest
How nightmares overgrow the dreamer's rest!
This thought engulfed in smiles her glowing face,
To sense how much her Presence could erase,
And that these so-called Keepers of the Flame
Were dumb to sorrow and its very name;
In fact, now found her choice of site quite 'smart':
So buzzards view a corpse as 'work of art'!
    Be that as well it may! Now came her take-off
Of Kansas Cooking Bee and Upstate Bake-off:
Two dozen ovens lent by Pillsbury Flour
Had been dispersed throughout that dismal bower;
The theme was 'Apples,' whether sauce or tart,
And US' Bards as only "Moms" at Heart'!
For this event, she posted prizes plenty:
The first, a hosted tour of San Clemente;
The next, our Rhinestone Scribes were pleased to know,
A 'guest shot' on the Johnny Carson Show!
Our Networks Three would air the whole shebang
By Telstar with official *Sturm und Drang*,
For what could assauge those hungry eyes

Like Existential Poets wasting pies?
As now they pounded dough and poured the batter
To give the famished world the things that matter,
The deep-dish mystic thrill, the riddle lean,
That live and breathe like us, not merely *mean*!
As Bishop† in her Dutch Maid's cap and dress
Like Molly Pitcher minced with nice finesse,
Advising all on measures and amounts,
Confiding quiet warnings: "Neatness counts!"
And Richard Kostelanetz leaned about
Admonishing: "Leave all the apples out!"††
The Goddess relished, licking-bowl in lap,
The smell of poets working: burning sap!
    The contest over, Koch's 'Raisin Snack'
Was given to the poor, who gave it back;
Joel Oppenheimer early lost the race,
As lofty cakes collapsed to lower case;
Giorno's 'pounder' weighed much more than pound,
Because it held a heavy boot he'd 'found';†††
H. Nemerov, adept at prankster jolts,
Had baked in his a box of nuts and bolts;
Saroyan†††† proved an overeager 'also ran,'
By using just an inch or two of pan;

---

†Poet Elizabeth Bishop.
††Richard Kostelanetz, literary gadfly and obsessive exponent of zany, alchemic experimentation with the physical appearance of 'poems' on the page. He is fond of quoting Dadaist Tzara's 'No more words' and other such dated and quixotic exhortations.
†††John Giorno, as stated, insists he's elevated so-called 'found poetry,' another contradiction in terms of misanalogy from the world of visual art, this time sculpture, to a fine art.
††††Aram Saroyan, arch-minimalist, suggesting a verse that might be added:
    "Lives of great men all remind us
    Their eager sons are sure to find us—"

While Justice† took defeat with solemn air,
Both held and ate his cake, a perfect square;
The Goddess gave MacLeish a grateful nudge
For sticking to his guns and making fudge;
And Alistair Reid,†† a 'limey' awf'ly 'in',
Brought down the house by lacing his with gin;
Bright Corso eyed the prize but could not nab it,
Not with those 'potted brownies' baked from habit;
At last, poor Moss engaged in great harangue
When Brinnin was dismissed for pure meringue;
King John, of course, as always, justly won:
His entry: empty pan entitled 'Bun'!
   Like noble Arthur over heath and weir,
John heralded his men toward Belvedere,†††
Where soon the critics' sessions would be held,
And reputations fed on those dispelled!
What pedant whose complacencies inure
A paltry soul to petty sinecure
Considers what 'degenerative change'
Has made his 'expertise' the poet's range,
When only recently was English 'taught,'
And people paid to 'teach' what poets 'thought.'††††
A most unnatural situation, that!
Instructing Dullness how to put on fat?
The bourgeois has forgotten in its plight,

---

†Donald Justice, the academic poet and middleman.
††Reid still has a wide following at Sarah Lawrence, where he once taight, and was known as quite a 'cut up.'
†††Belvedere Castle is a 'medieval' structure located north of the Ramble in Central Park. It stands upon a promontory above a small pond, or extended mud puddle, choked with broken glass and other rubbish.
††††Clara Claiborne Park, herself a teacher of English at Berkshire Community College, wrote in a review of a reissue of Ashbery's *Rivers and Mountains* by Ecco Press (*The Nation*, Sept. 3, 1977):

Just how to live, much less to read and write!
Beware, you pompous, high-paid verbal snobs,
Remember how you got those trumped-up jobs:
The fate that overtook the *ancien clerc*†
Will turn you out-of-doors and back to work!
It is a coil of opposites, the brain,
That once compressed as now, springs up again!
Old love and innocence and lively wine
Will meet again within the poet's line;
And verse, once more a Tigris in its course,
Will fuse our continents with massive force,
When liqueurs of the 'tongue' are not distilled
To 'bitters' for an epic unfulfilled!
    This 'haunting' thought, despite much 'macho' talk,
They won't accost along 'Old College Walk'!
Still, Bloom in tux, a beacon from the wall,††
Spread wide his arms, to greet, and upstage all!
The Goddess broadcast from the steep escarpment:

"It is more than a coincidence that these years of the steady contraction of poetry's public sector are also the years in which English literature became for the first time a subject of study. We should not forget that that seemingly immemorial entity, The English Department, did not exist before the 20th century. In no previous era was it a function of university teaching to train an audience for literature written in the mother tongue. Students in universities a hundred years ago did not study Shakespeare, or Pope, or the Romantic poets; still less did they study contemporary poetry. They did study Latin and Greek. . . . Poetry in English was not studied, but read. People who did not find reading it in some way enjoyable did not read it at all. There was no occasion to; one of the more interesting dates in literary history must be the date when someone was first graded on his reading of a poem."

---

†That truly concerned commentator and person, Dwight Macdonald, reminds us in his Preface to *Against the American Grain:* "The section entitled 'Traitors' is about what Julien Benda once called 'le trahison des clercs.' This is usually translated 'the treason of the intellectuals,' but the medieval term *clercs* is more what I mean; 'academics' is the closest modern English can come."
††Harold is poised upon the Castle parapet!

"He'll have his very own, complete Department,"
She baited them, "Who can make any sense
Of all the crap that will assail him hence!
Who gives the strangest *mis*-interpretation†
Will win a medal from 'a greatful nation'!
To those who've made our trade a rare disease,
My annual awards, the env'lopes, please!
To Kostelanetz, for his active part
In chopping verse up into 'visual art';††
To Kumar,††† whosoever he might be!
For absolutely nothing, seriously!
To Leonard, John, maestro of the 'zingers,'
My box of puns and 'Chinese lady fingers'!††††

---

†Hilton Kramer, commenting on the pretensions of Harold Bloom's critical posture, in the *New York Times Book Review*, August 21, 1977, writes: "Misreading the great poets, you see, is not for Professor Bloom a bad thing. It is quite a good thing. It is a marvelously creative thing. It is certainly to be recommended. The best poets are alleged to be doing it all the time. That's one of the ways we know that they *are* the best poets, it seems. So why shouldn't the critics too avail themselves of this unexpected privilege? Why should the poets have all the fun? Who among us can put his hand on his heart and honestly swear he knows what these infernal poets are up to, anyway? Not Professor Bloom. We have it on his own authority that in the criticism of literature 'there are no interpretations but only misinterpretations.' This is a wonderfully convenient theory. What vistas it opens! What feats of mind it promises! . . . For this new mode of free-wheeling misreading places the critic beyond the realm of truth and error, beyond all mundane plausibility."

††Richard Kostelanetz in his oppressive quest for cleverness and emblematic exoticism has edited a book, *Breakthrough Fictioneers*, which holds that the main justification for further writing might be the novelty of words, letters or other symbols scattered about the page for their visual, design effects.

†††Dr. Shiv K. Kumar is Professor of English at the University of Hyderabad and writes 'criticism' for *Span*, a U.S. Government periodical put out in India.

††††Chinese lady fingers' are dainty little firecrackers on a string. John Leonard could make his columns even more 'sprightly' with these, if that is at all conceivable!

To Mrs. Perloff† at poor USC,
The 'Moore Award'†† for 'preciosity';
For Vendler, Grumbach, †††those in Punch's stable,
My pledge: he'll grasp no more than Cain is able!
And last, for vet'ran booster William Cole,††††
My int'mate guide to 'foot-in-mouth' control!
To all of you, and many, many more,
Whose daily 'living' is a deadly bore,
I wish you, with my deepest, heartfelt 'thanks'!
The best of many 'dish days' at the banks!"
   With this, she 'threw it all' to mighty Bloom!
Who waved de Man††††† aside to make some room
And placed his students with their Yalie stripes
By height to either side like organ pipes,
And then for pear-shaped tones and breath control,
Did sev'ral knee-bends and a 'mattress roll,'
Turned-up the mike, and opened wide 'the bible,'
That tome of his entitled *Bloom's Large Libel*!
With this obnoxious, single, crack-pot book,
Hal ripped the ivy from its 'crannied nook'!
By claiming that 'misreadings'†††††† of the text

---

†Mrs. Marjorie Perloff, English Professor at the University of Southern California.
††Marianne Moore.
†††Helen Vendler and Doris Grumbach, whose poetry criticism toes the line for Young Punch Sulzberger's N.Y. *Times*. Some line!
††††*Trade Winds* Editor for Saturday Review of Literature and blurber-at-large.
†††††Paul de Man, one of Bloom's colleagues at Yale.
††††††To continue with Kramer from the *Times* piece quoted above:

"(Misreading) gives him (the critic) the freedom of his imagination. It makes him—dare one say it?—almost a poet. . . . The act of misreading, you see, is conceived to be part of a heroic and bloody battle. 'Reading is defensive warfare,' according to Professor Bloom. Therefore, criticism (his sort of criticism, anyway) acquires (in his eyes, anyway) all the drama of a life of

Would help us tell one critic from the next!
Contempt for sense, he said, would make them stoic;
The worse the error, O, the more heroic!
If poets could defy coherent recall,
Let chaos then become the end and be-all!
To hell with Keats' careful separation
Of 'fancy' from a 'true imagination':
They find such differentiations slight,
As cats see only grey both day and night,
And claim this gross, psychotic, mass condition
Some kind of new, disposable tradition,
Where critics can outply the poet's plow
In nullity, or as he put it now:
"If poets with their cryptic stance, confound it!
Cop all the prizes, critics *must* compound it!"
Bloom fumed! "We'll out-ellipse and out-abstruse them!
Out-loop! Out-smoke! Out-shame! *And* out-traduce them!
Which I have done, to give you *one* example,
And worried forth these pearls, which now you'll sample!"
    His colleagues gathered at the Castle's foot
Like fragile leaves to his one branch and root!
First rapt, as Paul along Damascus Road,
Then lashed to fury as by cattle-goad!
As Bloom declaimed, in wild, 'belated'† glory

combat in the trenches. What a farce! Who would have thought that literary criticism, of all things, would one day be promoted as the moral equivalent of war? One doesn't know whether to laugh or cry at the thought of all those docile undergraduates in New Haven being force-fed this nonsense. What a ruinous way to make an acquaintance with serious literature!"

†One of Bloom's contentions is that the poet's desperation comes from the fact that some other poet 'said it first.' This also afflicts critics, who can compensate for it, Bloom says, through the originality of their contributions, which of course in his case might be called a kind of eccentricity, or, to give the point a little room to run around in, madness!

The utter nonsense of an Irwin Cory!†
And acolytes, resounding to the slopes,
Compounded compounds of his compound tropes!
While Ginsberg and the crowd from Old Naropa
Brought hands to face in holy 'ropa-dopa'!††
Assumed the lotus or the pretzel stance,
As strangely now arose their *Om*-like chants:
The *Oms* of Krishna or the Maharani,
Mixed with the West Side *Oms* of D. Kermani!†††
At last the Goddess in her rapture stood,
And breathed, "In comes the bad, out goes the good!"
And Muses, *Om*, with plastic flag and torch,
Did 'modern dance' 'o'er ramparts that we watch'!
They came, the *Oms*, they came, as night set in,
With whips of rain, they came, and lightning's din!
Now every lip vibrated with the hum
And filled the grove with sounds of locusts come!
The Bronx was burning, *Om*, the radio said,
And *Om* just bubbled from the many dead!
And still it swept, that *Om*'s uncanny tone,
The crowd, a chimney flue, with wintry moan!
Old Nelson's 'horns,' or 'tusks,'†††† they say, were struck!
Now *Om* met *Clang* aboard the ladder-truck!
And Brooklyn, *Om*, had been engulfed in flame!
Or was it Queens? *Om* smiled: It's all the same!

---

†TV's nonsense comic, Professor Irwin Cory.
††The Buddhist hand-to-face in prayer somewhat resembles Ali's cover-up along the ropes, which he calls his 'ropa-dope.'
†††*Self-Portrait in a Convex Mirror* is dedicated to David Kermani, who was there that night, taking notes on what Bloom had to say about John Ashbery, which has consistently been, if tentative, in keeping with Bloom's oracular station, always lauditory.
††††Henceforth, let's call The Twin Towers of the World Trade Center Nelson's 'horns,' for they will surely do him in. Or in keeping with the current reference to them as the multi-billion dollar 'white elephants,' Nelson's 'tusks'! History in the making, eh?

Then *Om* was shaken by a mighty shout!
Bloom reached his point, just as the lights went out!
Om met the monster called Con Edison,
But had no stomach for Con's medicine!
Poor *Om* went down, no more to say about it,
And all went home to hum and pray about it!

Epilogue

So, Harry! Home, at last! Now may I beg,
Does 'Old Nantucket' still break out a keg?
And does its ancient welcome yet extend
To those confounded by the journey's end?
Whose sails outpiled the perils of the world,
Then fell accurst, by that rude Goddess furled!
Yes, home! But not for long! Then out again
To where we left her, which I will explain!
Eight months at sea! Now is that time enough
To warrant rations and a pinch of snuff,
When Dullness keeps her troops on so much more
For simple sallies to the kitchen door?
This trip has fattened up the child in me!
He knows I spend adrenalin at sea,
And stay too late among the star-stretched hours
And stare too far beyond the sea-fed flowers,
And now he makes me drink for any sake,
Contempt for evil or the love of Blake,

Commutes the sentence, death, to days of booze,
Then lets me serve the time as I would choose,
Until my mind a distant pin attends
Where still the pendulum of stars depends!
  The business of her kingdom crams my ear,
And I must shake the sea to think or hear!
Shocked, stunned by what I saw, unclothed, I stand!
So stripped of all the habits of the land,
Put-off by all the costumes of the day,
Unmoved by all the outcomes of the play,
A shadow in the masque of moon and night,
Until the dawn redress my naked sight,
And I re-enter for a shave and rub
By rites of passage in a steaming tub,
And am myself again, or seem the same,
As he who left here with accustomed name!
Should from my utterance then stumble out
Some blatant outcry or some troubled shout,
Some echo of the sphere, to her oblate,
Where Dullness pickles Mankind for her plate,
Insinuates the guile of her dominion
Through every devil's hump and angel's pinion,
That as we shrug or hope for 'all the best,'
Observe our clocks and credos, all the rest,
Deal right or wrong, renege, proceed to play,

Say black is white, recant, swear both are grey,
Conspire, withdraw, commit, conform, refute,
Our stubborn action is her strongest suit!
Complacency and fear, her potent wares,
Suborn our consciences to Trojan mares:
Besieged by contradictions from within,
Where most we strive, the least we stand to win;
With Chile, Cuba, Nam or Mayaguez,
Committed strength collapses to malaise!
A culture lacking universal gist
Is bound, a man strung-up, to gibber, twist,
And stare whichever way the wind has blown,
Until the blade of his'try cuts it down!
   On either side of ev'ry mortal plot,
She's active where 'assuredly' she's not:
Who seeks his refuge in the desert air
Is bound to find her with another there,
And soon a great metropolis crops up,
Where but to pass is to become corrupt!
Yet there are sunlit times and secret places
Where innocence defies her sullen traces:
She dreads naivete and happenstance,
Insouciance and the statue's careless glance,
The unclaimed dead, a child, a sheltered barn,
A lighted face, all find her put upon;

Where nature might unfold in man or tree,
She will not interpose or deign to be;
Where men are honest and the rivers flow,
She will not venture forth or dare to go;
A piercing eye she fears at ev'ry frolic,
As felons loathe the light, and vampires, garlic!
Regard this frown, the level of my eyes,
The measure of her swiftly moving guise:
It is the line against her I have drawn,
The impress of horizons where I've gone,
To cauterize the poet's severed sight
And pierce her chaos and impending night!
    And still I must restore these scattered bones
To native shores and smooth Nantucket stones:
To Father Mapple through the ocean's cleft,
We bring the sign he gave us when we left!
We bore it well through each abysmal strait,
A key to Heaven? No, Nantucket's gate!
It was a voice beside us where we went,
A Presence ever active, never spent,
As hell is restless in these avid eyes
And little seashells whisper 'paradise!'
His blessing binds us to that doubtful end
Of common God and Ev'ryman as friend,
To build a mighty kingdom of our loss

That has no lock or key, hence needs no cross!
So ask him if his sermon now will keep
Until we fix accounts and get some sleep.
For we have wandered far and wander still
From thoughts we left upon that Boeotian sill,
Where last we saw the Goddess and her horde,
At what? I guess, with time thrown overboard!
   My premature return with half a hold,
My swift recourse to port with much untold,
Is all the proof and evidence you need,
To send us out again with utmost speed!
Her forces you must know are strong and trim,
Who could subvert our plan by printer's whim,
And so foreclose our preconceived design
To trap her final acts within our line;
So like a brand or fad she spread his name
That we must rush to print to meet his fame,
Before she finds another Dunce's face
To be her trademark in the market-place!
How like her mind, to make us capsulate,
The kind of vast apocalyptic fate
I heard her prophet Bavius ordain,
To close the planet down with King John's reign!
It may be more than deadlines that we meet;
Her Armageddon that we go to greet!

If Pope could warn, "She comes, she comes!" O, fear!
May we not say at last, "She's here, she's here!"
    You'd think so if you tracked her to that shore,
Her poets draped like addicts on each oar,
And watched her hatch her plots upon that isle,
To blow us all to hell for quite a while!
That Bavius, as Pope had pictured him,
Her serpent and the Dunce's paradygm,
Fell to his knees at just the sight of John,
And found his face a jew'l to dote upon!
"My boy," he wept, "the Lethe flows more verily
To bathe in you the better part of me!†
Your Queen has urgent, utter need of you!
Destroy their senses and the rest we'll do!
O, trumpets! Drums! The moment and the man!
The happy husband of her monstrous plan!
And what a handsome salesman to promote
To national pastime his poetic trope,
To turn our language into gibberish,
Implying all or nothing as you wish;
Indeed, to make the practice seem perverse,
Beyond the college wall, a kind of curse;
A great derangement of the normal brain
That holds a lack of life its one refrain!
How well you've kept the middle classes smitten

---

†Bavius was an ancient poet satirized by Virgil very much as Cibber was by
Pope. Bavius was so effectively despised that his native isle of Boeotia became
famous for dullness. Pope (see *The Dunciad*, Book the Third) imagines Bavius,
in league with the Goddess, baptizing prior to their birth, in the Lethe, those
souls who will live their mortal lives as Dunces.

With poems whose subject is the way they're written;
Go, bid their expectation lift its glass,
Then leave it quaintly empty as you pass;
Go, challenge them, then strike reaction dead,
As blows assault the unsuspecting head!
Called Existentialism, eh? Uncanny!
A catchword for the market, sharp as any!"
   "O, Bavius" the Goddess stamped, "Go hence!
You just confuse him with attempts at sense:
Now John," she spoke, "We've brought to fever pitch
The bourgeois ego and the banker's itch;
Two-thousand years we've spent to lay these fuses,
Reduce the multitudes to all my uses,
To make the many nations all my cults
Until they cry for uniform results,
And everyone right down to Billy Graham
Has his or her investment in my mayhem!
Now we're prepared to push the final plunger
And put an end to universal hunger,
To get this cosmic show upon the road
And blow it all to bits to ease the load!
Now wouldn't you enjoy just taking part
And in the ruins firing up your art?
Of course you would! Just do as you are told,
And Johnny Dim becomes King John the Bold!
It's best when all the world is turning dumb

To follow simple, handy rules of thumb!
In driving Mankind down the path of hell,
To reassure him all is going well,
That hell is just a home away from home,
Your verse, another kind of harmless poem!
Just void his mind while filling up his ear,
Like Musak while he's in the dentist's chair!
We must not interrupt the media noise,
Nor tolerate the kind of counterpoise
That poets offered once in brash defiance,
To all my arts of money, war and science!
Through you we automate the rule of Dunce:
Usurp the poet's role, pre-empt response,
Tie-up the presses, satisfy the set,
Relax the prey, and then we drop the net!"
    That's when I left them, knowing I must go!
Had Dullness, or the printer, planned it so?
Is this much epic equal to the store
Of half a loaf where there was none before?
Like Howitzers aloft the great gale hurdles
Beyond the steeple where the ocean curdles,
And time is of the essence, days not years,
Like dying flames, attenuate our fears,
And I attend the ending of the tale,
As Ishmael remembered Ahab's whale!

finis